SPIRIT,
SOUL
&
BODY

SPIRIT, SOUL & BODY

Which Way Are You *Leaning*?

Today's decisions are tomorrow's destinies...

Allen McCroskey

Some illustration content used in this book was created by Presentermedia.com / Sioux Falls, SD

Editor: Amelia Bozeman

Allen McCroskey
Nashville, TN
URSpiritSoulBody@gmail.com

Printed in the United States of America

Contents

FOREWORD

by Jim Frease

Founder and senior pastor of Joy Church as well as founder and president of World Changers Bible Institute in Mt. Juliet, TN.

"Spirit, Soul & Body"

You may have heard the phrase in Christian circles, "In Christ" or "You just have to know who you are in Christ", as some Christians will emphatically tell you. Unfortunately, most believers don't understand what these phrases mean. Simply put, seeing yourself "in Christ" means "how God sees you because of what Jesus Christ has done for you."

In Allen McCroskey's new book, "Spirit, Soul & Body", Allen helps you unlock this extremely vital truth. If Christians don't understand that they are a spirit, they have a soul, and they live in a body, much of the Christian's life will be much like a roller coaster...up one day and down the next.

I personally learn in a much more effective manner through pictures. Jesus taught this way through parables. The Greek word for parable is "parabole". This is a Greek compound word. "Para" which means "to come alongside", and "bole" which means to "throw down". Put these Greek words together and it tells us that Jesus used word pictures called 'parables' to come alongside a spiritual truth and throw down a picture. These pictures were designed by Jesus to enhance our learning process. I love this refreshing element in Allen's book as he includes little pictures to help illustrate very important spiritual truths.

Lastly, I have personally known Allen for many years, and he is one of the most encouraging, generous, loving and Christ-like people I know! Because I think so highly of the author, it automatically lends credibility to his work. I highly recommend both Allen McCroskey and his wonderful new book, "Spirit, Soul & Body"!

1

Introduction:

Christianity is not another religion to choose. It is an actual relationship with God made possible through His precious Son named Jesus, living, and growing like a seed inside you. This seed is in the form of the Holy Spirit and resides in the spirit of every born-again believer. When you discover that we were created in God's image and are comprised of three parts like Him, your understanding in all areas of the Bible will take off!

Man is a tri-part being. Realizing that we are a spirit, we have a soul, and that we live in an earth suit called the body, many principles taught through the Bible will have far greater meaning and come alive to you. I know of nothing that will unlock your understanding of God's Word more than comprehending how He made us to operate as a tri-being. "We are fam-i-ly..." We all are born *through* our mother, with physical attributes, but *from* God with His Spiritual DNA. This study will open your mind to foundational questions like, "What does it mean to walk in the Spirit?" or "If I am really saved, why don't I feel like it?" So, get ready to take a journey into the *"real you"*!

When God created you and me, He decided to make us in His image. On the last day of creation, God said, "Let us make man in our image, in our likeness" (Genesis 1:26). After He had created man, He then breathed His breath into man giving us the ability to be a *speaking spirit*. (Genesis 2:7). Accordingly, man is unique among all God's creations, having both a material body and an immaterial soul/spirit. You are God's crown jewel and have so much value that He paid the ultimate price for you, His only son Jesus Christ!

To help more deeply understand the life changing truths about the real you, this book is chock full of illustrations to help you *get the picture* of a scripture or verses in the Bible. Since our minds thinks in pictures, when vivid pictures accompany someone's words, the understanding and retention of that subject goes up astoundingly. Jesus used word picture analogies to help create the correct mental pictures in people's minds so that they could understand a concept or lesson more quickly.

As you read through the pages of this book you will see in pictures that out of all creation, we are God's masterpiece and crown jewel! We were created and have the ability to succeed in every area of our lives. Illustrations in this book will open your eyes to truths that you are a spirit, you possess a soul, and you live in a body. Jesus took complicated things and made them simple while religion takes simple things and makes them hard. When you can more fully understand the purpose God has for us and the abilities He has provided in our spiritual backpack, your life will never be the same. You will no longer be a well without water or a cloud without life giving rain! Your mind will be transformed from the inside out!

CHAPTER 1

Jesus taught in pictures!

Jesus taught in pictures. Imagine Him saying, "You want to know about faith? Here's a mustard seed. You want to know about what it means to be a servant? Let me show you a child." That's what a parable is, a *word picture!* It says come alongside me and I'll lay down a story about a spiritual principle.

We have all certainly heard the phrase "A picture paints a thousand words." Pictures often describe things more easily than words. I believe that this is because they appeal to the imagination part that God instilled into each of us so that we could see further. Words produce images in our spirits and in our minds.

He created the human eyes to see. He created our spirit and soul to have vision and to be able to imagine and have dreams of things we can do and accomplish for Him with our lives. God knew that a parable would project the correct word picture in our minds so that we would remember the lesson. It is His Word that helps us to develop the correct image of the unseen within us. If something is physically seen it is subject to change! We can take God's Word and change the things that are seen with the things we desire that are unseen. This Is the reason it is important to not let our physical eyes see wrong images.

Proverbs 4:25
"Keep your eyes focused on what is right and look straight ahead to what is good."

Therefore, it is so important to never gaze at what you do not want in your future. Whatever your mind focuses on will grow larger. Where the mind goes the man will follow. Do you see how this could help or hurt you to prosper in the things of God?

Remembering in Pictures

Have you ever forgotten someone's name but a week or month later you still remembered his or her face? We all have experienced that, but why? When you have a dream, if you happened to remember what it was about, did it come to you in abstract words or pictures? Pictures, right? That is how our minds communicate with us.

If I were to ask you to think about a big black dog, what immediately popped up in your mind? Was it the words BIG BLACK DOG or was it the picture? If I add the word growling to the big, black dog, what happens? The picture goes from static to animation but the letters in growling do not appear in your mind. It is difficult to retain just words with facts and figures, but you will remember a story much more easily because it paints a flowing connected picture.

If I were to ask you to tell me how many windows were in your home, you would not immediately know that answer. However, if you used the imagination of your mind, you could count each one because you have seen the picture many times. Go ahead, give it a try! This is exactly how architects design buildings and inventors invent things that have never been built, they see them in their imaginations. David said in 1 Chronicles 29:18, "keep this forever in the imagination of their mind". If you have ever given someone directions to your house, you saw the streets and traffic lights in your mind.

Radio sports reporters have used descriptive words for decades in hopes of taking us there visually in our minds with some success. However, when viewing actual pictures to a story, the story has far greater impact for the viewer who was not there to see further into what really happened. Since people really think in pictures, adding a picture in a story jumpstarts the ability for the mind to imagine and understand more quickly ideas, concepts, places, and people. Television accomplished that to *tell a vision*. The word was derived from *tele* meaning far and *visio* meaning sight.

We see innovations online which allow text to be mixed with pictures and have enabled companies like YouTube and Instagram to be widely accepted social media exchanges. They realize that pictures help us take in information so much more quickly than we could ever have before! Rather than having to read a story or see a static picture, we can almost be there to get a full picture of what happened with a video. This is also the reason that video emails are popular in marketing because they understand that the quicker the connection for the viewer to see the benefit, the sooner they will accept the product.

People do not see life as *it is*, they see life as *they are*. Your perception is your reality! If you lived out your life primarily with only a view from the outward man, meaning your body, we would go by what we could feel, see, taste, touch, or smell.

With just a little knowledge about the subject of your imagination, it's likely that you are already understanding how important and powerful the images and pictures you view are to you and your future. Wouldn't it be important to sit down and use our imagination to see ourselves accomplishing good things in life?

The goal of this book is to provide you with a picture that goes along with words and helps you more easily see the benefit of a principle or lesson from God. When our minds are opened to the correct images it is easier to accept the product (His Son Jesus and the all the benefits). The amazing thing that happens, is that the more you understand what God is saying to you, the more you will understand how much He is in love with us and wants us to prosper! My favorite verse is Jeremiah 29:11 which says,

"For I know the plans I have for you," declares the LORD, "plans to prosper you and not harm you, plans to give you hope and a future."

In this verse, God is giving us an open canvas for Him to paint a picture of what hope is (in our hearts), so that we may be all that He has created us to be! If you saw a painting by the world-famous painter Rembrandt and could only see the bottom right corner where he placed his signature, you would know that it was a gem. Rembrandt's paintings created memorable action scenes where the actors depicted appeared to be alive with movement.

Visualize for a moment your life painting. What if only the lower right corner of the painting was showing, and you saw God's signature in red? As you lived your life and your painting was revealed day by day, would it be painted with *your* apparent movement for Him? Would you read and believe what He thinks about you? Without doubt, He only paints masterpieces but here is what's most important: He allows you to direct the daily brush strokes of His hand over the course of your life. Isaiah 45:11 says, "Command Me concerning the work of My hands."

God-Eternity past

This literally means that as believers, we have the ability to pray in faith according to any promise in His Word and direct its release into our life painting. How does this happen? Since God has already restored every born-again believer through His grace and faith through Jesus, we have authority to operate according to His Word and His backing. When our prayers *of faith* line up with His promises, it is done! He does this as an expression of His love for us and the relationship we have with Him through His Son Jesus. It is a privilege to command His Hand, and if exercised with fervent respectful petition, there is nothing that will be impossible to the believer. If you first read what His promises are for you and then use your imagination to create movement, your own masterpiece will unfold incrementally day by day. You cannot do anything in your physical body that has not first occurred in your mind. The good news is that we can choose our thoughts. This means we do not have to think about whatever negative thought that drops into our minds. Successful movement is aiming your imagination in the right direction plus daily action so that you can reach toward your full potential! "Faith without works is dead." (James 2:17) Your imagination gives you a visualization of what can be so that you have a roadmap to work toward *by faith*!

So, let's dive into a few pictures to give us a visual of just how God created us! I believe these pictures will change your life forever.

Chapter 2

The Stuff They Don't Teach You in Church

God made us for a purpose, and we are His masterpiece! We are each uniquely created by Him for specific tasks and at a specific time. His perfect will for us is our calling. A career and calling are not necessarily the same thing. While the career you have now is what you do, your calling is what God really called you to do. If both are the same for you, great! If you have second thoughts that they are not both the same, then here are just a few of these scriptures that will get your thinking started:

- Ecclesiastes 3:1 says, "There is an appointed time for everything. And there is a time for every event under heaven."
- Romans 12:1-2, Paul tells us that we are to not be conformed to this world, but to present our bodies as a living sacrifice to God.
- Ephesians 1:11 "In him we have obtained an inheritance, having been predestined according to the purpose of him who works all things according to the counsel of his will." We each have been given unique talents and promises in our backpack from God to use for Him! What would you do *for free* if you were financially independent? That may be your calling.
- Ephesians 2:10, For we are his workmanship, created in Christ Jesus for good works, which God prepared beforehand, that we should walk in them.
- Jeremiah 29:11 "For I know the plans I have for you, declares the Lord, plans for good and not for evil, to give you a future and hope.
- Isaiah 43:7 states "Everyone who is called my name who I created for My glory, who I formed and made." We fulfill our purpose of glorifying God by our relationship with Him and through faithful service. The

more we glorify the Lord the more we understand how much He loves us and how He created us to function.

One of the most touching scriptures that spell out the forethought God had for each of us in the Bible comes from David.

"My frame was not hidden from You, when I was made in secret, and skillfully wrought I the lowest parts of the earth. Your eyes saw my substance, being yet unformed. And in Your book, they all are written, the days fashioned for me, when as yet there were none of them." Psalm 139:15-16

Think about that for just a moment with me. God looked at each of us individually and His eyes saw our substance. That is worth getting excited about!

Let's look at how it all happened. A good starting point for us would be in the book of Genesis to find out how we were created. Here we find initial phases of how the world came into existence along with the elements and creatures that inhabit the Earth.

First: Your body was formed...

"And the Lord God formed man of the dust of the ground...."

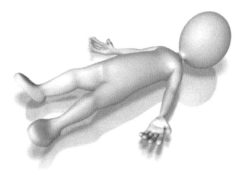

(Genesis 2:7)

The word *formed* in this scripture is from the Hebrew word "Yâtsar." It means to squeeze into shape, mold, and form as a potter. *1 The body was formed from dirt which was something that already existed. It is a house or vessel for the Soul.

Second: Your soul was created...

... "and breathed into his nostrils the breath of life; and man became a living Soul." The Hebrew word for Adam is Aw-Dawn which means man, rosy-to show blood in the face. (Genesis 2:7)

When God breathed the breath of life into the body, it made the body, soul, and spirit live and function together. *2

Third: Your spirit was created!

"So God created him in His own image in the image of God created He him, male and female created he them." (Genesis 1:27)

It is important to note as you read the word that our body was formed from something that pre-existed which was dirt. But as God finished man, His masterpiece creation, He created our soul and spirit with words of faith.

The first two chapters of Genesis are generally referred to as the creation chapters. As God was finishing His creation, He caused fish to come into existence by speaking to the water, so fish were derived from the substance of water. God then created animals by speaking to the earth, so animals were derived from the substance of the Earth. Look closely at how God changed course when He created man. God Created Man by speaking to Himself so that our core substance is derived directly from God! We have God's own Spirit as a part of who we are which makes us different from any other living creature in the world.

And God said, Let us make *man in our image, after our likeness: and let them have dominion over the fish of the sea, and over the fowl of the air, and over the cattle, and over all the earth, and over every creeping thing that creepeth upon the earth. So, God created man in His own image, in the image of God created He him; male and female created he them.* **(Genesis 1:26-27)**

So, God made us in His image and after His likeness. This means that we are a snapshot of God and were made to resemble Him in many respects.

Then God blessed them and said, 'Be fruitful and multiply. Fill the earth and govern it. Reign over the fish in the sea, the birds in the sky, and all the animals that scurry along the ground.'" (Genesis 1:28)

Although we have elements of the earth that make up our bodies, the core of who we are is our *spirit*. We have God's DNA within our spirit man and a position of "oversight" as well. Therefore, it was God's intent explained in Genesis that we have dominion over the whole earth. In other words, *He gave Adam and Eve management instructions and handed them the keys.*

You Are Made Up of Three Distinct Parts!

In 1 Thessalonians 5:23 we find evidence that we are made of these three distinct elements:

"And the very God of peace sanctify you wholly; and I pray God your whole spirit, soul, and body be preserved blameless unto the coming of our Lord Jesus Christ."

From this verse we begin to see clearly that we are made from three parts which are the spirit, soul, and body. To be a little more specific, we *are* a spirit, we *have* a soul, and we *live* in a body. All three of these parts are linked together in that order.

Spirit   Soul   Body

Another way to explain these three parts for a born-again believer (someone who has made the decision to accept Jesus as their Lord and Savior) would be to say:

Spirit: Who you are in Christ

Soul: Who you are in your mind, will & emotions (your personality)

Body: Who you are in your physical appearance

Chapter 3

The Most Extravagant Gift

The book of Genesis describes to us multiple times that all of what God created on the earth was good. After God said, "Let us make man in our image and after our likeness: and let them have dominion..." man became a living soul and was clothed with God's glory and light. (Genesis 1:26) Psalm 8:5 says, "You made him (man) a little lower (physically) than the heavenly beings (angels) and crowned him (or clothed him) with glory and honor."

God himself empowered Adam and later his wife Eve to walk in blessing and prosperity in the garden of Eden. The garden of Eden was God's family project for Adam and Eve to serve as good stewards. With God's own spirit living on the inside of them, they were to be the builders, caretakers, and property managers to expand Eden eventually around the whole planet. When they expanded Eden, they would also be expanding God's presence around the earth.

How would they have dominion and expand the garden around the planet? We expand God's presence when we submit and follow God's Word. Since we are the image of God on earth, as are fruitful and multiply, we expand His image wherever we go. The rest of the earth was not in the same condition as the Garden of Eden, but God created it with that potential. God did not create Adam and Eve and their descendants to be servants *of* the earth, but lords *over* the earth with the authority and dominion he gave them.

The freedom to enjoy God's garden of Eden plus the benefits of being filled with God in their spirit, soul and body came with five commands, with the last one being different by having a penalty attached.

- Be fruitful
- Multiply

- Replenish the earth
- Have dominion over the earth, cultivate it, and tend it
- Do not eat from the tree of knowledge of good and evil

(Genesis 2:16-17)

"And the Lord God commanded the man, saying, 'Of every tree of the garden thou mayest freely eat: But the tree of knowledge of good and evil, thou shalt not eat of it: for in the day that thou eatest thereof thou shall surely die.'"

Here comes one of the biggest revelations of all time: God gave Adam and Eve their own free will! He gave you and me the ability to choose, making us all free agents in life. God did not create us as mindless robots to only do what He programmed us to do. How special is it to you, for your young child to climb into your lap and give you a hug just because they chose to do so, rather because you told them? Similarly, God's desire if for us to freely *choose* to love Him out of our own free will.

Adam and Eve had a tempter in the garden called the devil, that came in the form of a serpent. They were commanded by God to have dominion but regrettably, Eve was deceived. Adam followed suit and then blamed it all on her to God. They used their free will to do what Satan told them to do instead of obeying God. In bowing their knees to Satan, and by eating from the tree of knowledge of good and evil, they turned over their authority God had given them. Adam and Eve made Satan the illegitimate ruler of the earth, and in essence handed him over the keys.

Sadly, for the most part, many Christians falsely accuse or blame God for being the source of their troubles and deceived due to our human nature. They believe the lie that says, trials and tribulations are sent from God for developing strength and character.

Deception is the devil's tactic to cause us to doubt God's truths so that he may steal, kill, and destroy. "The thief cometh not, but for to steal, and to kill, and to destroy: I am come that they might have life, and that they might have *it* more abundantly. "(John 10:10) His only hope to control people is to get them to believe a lie, and he does it so subtly as to make it almost seem true. The best way to disguise a lie is to wrap it in truth. However, a lie wrapped in some part of truth is still a lie.

It is our free will that we choose and make daily decisions that lead us to our destinies. The good news is that we do not have to fall prey to areas of deception if we will guard our hearts daily with the light of truth from God.

Although Adam and Eve submitted to what the devil said instead of God's command, they did not experience immediate physical death, however they both died spiritually that day. The light of God's glory that they once walked in was snuffed out when they bowed to the devil and handed over the keys to him as the new property manager. From that moment on, the devil was given a greater advantage to try and bring sin, sickness, and poverty to mankind.

Adam's state of being *before The fall*

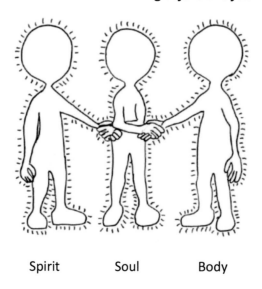

Spirit   Soul   Body

Adam was spiritually alive and connected with God. He was flawless in his spirit, soul, and body; he was made 100% perfect. He was illuminated with a full knowledge of God and His goodness. Adam's spirit man was the core of his being, and his soul and body were in sync. As a result, God's glory and blessings flowed like a river of living water to all three parts.

Adam's state of being *after The fall*

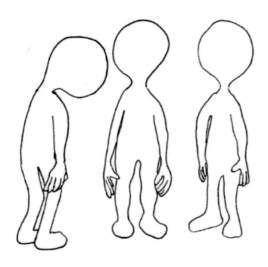

Spirit	Soul	Body
Tainted spirit man with a conscience and limited information from God	Restricted information	Lost immortality

Adam experienced spiritual death the moment he first sinned. His spirit man, the core of his being, became immediately tainted and inoperable the way it was prior. The glory of God that resided in him, left his spirit, soul, and body. For this reason, Adam and Eve realized that they were naked. The illumination (glory) they once had was gone and they hid because of their new sin consciousness.

But God had a plan... Jesus!

When Jesus hung on the cross, He literally *became* sin for us. Jesus became sickness, disease, lack, and poverty, so we would not have to endure these things without remedy. *Galatians 3:13-14* says, "Christ has redeemed us from the curse of the law, being made a curse for us; for it is written, cursed is every one that hangeth on a tree."

In *II Corinthians 5:21* we learn "For He that made Him to be sin for us, who knew no sin, that we might be made the righteousness of God in Him."

Jesus became our sin on the cross so that we could be in right standing with God through faith in Him! If He was willing to give you Christ, He is willing to freely give you every good thing. (Romans 8:32)

Righteousness cannot be earned through good conductor works; it is only received as a free gift through faith in Jesus. You will be happy to know that there are no levels of righteousness. We cannot buy our position of righteousness because it is free! When you understand that Jesus died just for you and you personally receive the precious gift of salvation, your spirit man becomes reborn and created brand new!

Come and Dine

The church that we attend has a regularly planned free buffet dinner for interested visitors to learn a little more about who we are. It is an opportune time to meet our pastors and several other members in a smaller more casual setting so that visitors can grow to understand more about us and the mission of our church. We always have a good number of people who respond and sign up for this nice dinner.

When our guests arrive at the home of one of our members, there are name badges laid out for them to wear to make it easier to meet and greet everyone. With about 30 guests registered each time, it is not uncommon for someone to be absent for one reason or another. Even though they were invited and had intentions of coming, not everyone chose to come and receive. That analogy is like the call that Jesus gives to each of us throughout our lives. He tells us to come and dine so that we can learn and understand how much He loves us. Jesus paid the price of sin for the whole world, but not everyone will choose to come and receive.

The good news today for those who have made the decision to accept the invitation from Jesus to be their Lord, is that as a believer in Christ, God's glory has been restored to you. You are a child of God and you have been accepted because of the sacrifice that Jesus paid for you! Therefore, you can boldly come before the Lord: because He sees you as He sees Jesus. In Matthew 16:19 Jesus speaks, "I will give unto thee the *keys of the kingdom of heaven;* and whatsoever thou shall bind on earth shall be bound in heaven; and whatsoever thou shall loose on earth shall be loosed in heaven".

Jesus has given you back the *master key* to your life. He offers *forgiveness* so you may be made free form the bondage of sin. God has given us His most extravagant gift...His very own Son!

Jesus died for the ungodly. While we were still sinners, He took our place and accepted the penalty of death for our sins. For this reason, God is no longer mad at us.... He is madly in Love with us!*1 We have been reconciled to God by the death of His Son. Jesus paid the price! By grace (Jesus paying the price), through faith (our acceptance of Jesus for the price He paid), we receive Jesus's 100% test score to enter Heaven when our life here ends.

We can learn to accept Jesus by hearing the Word of God regarding His Truths. Spiritual faith and understanding of this truth build on the inside of our soul man when we are continuing hearing His Word and renew our mind to its truths.

It might look something like this:

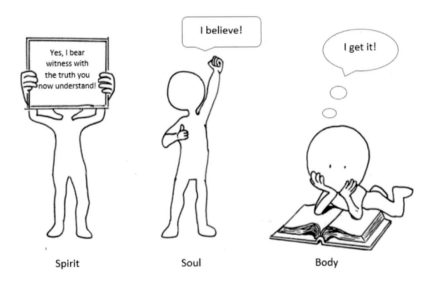

Spirit   Soul   Body

When you take time to renew your mind with the Word of God, you will notice in the illustration above that your spirit man, soul man and body are in agreement. Everyone is participating! Everything in life starts with a decision and then is followed by an action. Your soul man first decides to open the Bible which is spirit and life. You direct your body to use its eyes to read or ears to hear and consider what God's Word says. Once you renew your mind (soul) to what the Word of God says by bringing your body into subjection, the voice of your conscience in your spirit man that is prompted by the Holy Spirit jumps in and says, "Hey, you guys are correct!" Your spirit man, which already contains truth and the mind of Christ, bears witness to what you just read.

"I say the truth in Christ, I lie not, my conscience also bearing me witness in the Holy Spirit." **(Romans 9:1)**

This alignment between the soul and spirit is explained this way in **(1 John 5:6-10.):**

"He that believeth on the Son of God hath the witness in himself"

Our physical eyes are the windows of our souls. Renewing your mind (soul) by actually looking at the Word and reading it gives light about a situation, in a way that we can understand.

"The entrance of thy Word giveth light, it giveth understanding unto the simple." **(Psalm 119:130)**

The first thing you look for when you enter a dark room is the light switch. Stopping to look at the answer gives us insight so that we do not walk around in the dark stumbling into things. Even a small child knows and understands this.

The progression of reading the Word goes from believing to perceiving. The Bible calls us world overcomers. "For whatsoever is born of God overcometh the world: and this is the victory that overcometh the world, even our faith." **(1 John 5:4)** In the Old Testament, David was anointed king by the prophet Samuel when he was a teenager, but it was many years later before it finally sunk in that he would rule over Israel. The full realization and understanding came to David in 1 Chronicles 14:2: "And David perceived that the Lord had confirmed him king over Israel, for his kingdom was lifted up on high, because of his people Israel."

Jesus never said, "I feel" when relating to others; He used the word *perceived*. He was more in tune with His Spirit than He was with His body. Look how this would read if we changed the verb in Luke 8:46 to *feel*.

FEEL: "And Jesus said, 'Somebody hath touched me; for I *feel* that virtue is gone out of me.'"

PERCEIVE: "And Jesus said, 'Somebody hath touched me; for I *perceive* that virtue is gone out of me.'"

As you progress through these chapters, you will begin to perceive that you too are a world overcomer and already righteous in your spirit man. One of the first steps to perceiving who you are in Christ is having your soul man *in agreement* with what is in your spirit man. This allows truth to be received and manifestation to occur immediately or at least start growing in our souls and bodies. This manifestation can come in many forms.

First it starts with your *old spirit man* and creates in you a totally *new spirit*. God comes to live on the inside of your new spirit man in the form of the Holy Spirit.

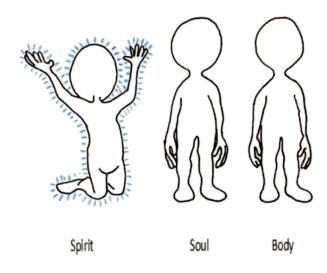

Spirit   Soul   Body

Mark explains this with his analogy of the new wine versus old wineskins.

"And no man puts new wine into old bottles: else the new wine does burst the bottles, and the wine is spilled, and the bottles will be marred: but new wine must be put into new bottles." **(Mark 2:22)**

New fermenting wine is placed in new wineskins because new wine expands. Therefore, old wineskins cannot be useful for new wine because they would burst with all the expansion. Likewise, God gives us a new spirit with unlimited capacity so that His glory and blessings can be forever expanding in our newly created spirits!

Do you have an area of lack in your life?

What area of your life is in lack? If you renew your mind to the promises of healing, then you are preparing the way for healing to come and manifest in your body. Renewing your mind to God's Word in the area of finances puts you on the right road to prosperity manifesting in your life. As you continue to open your mind to understanding spirit, soul, and body, you will begin to see that provision is already ours through the price that Jesus paid on the cross. Our responsibility is to understand how to receive what has already been done for us through Christ in every area of our lives.

"But He was wounded for our transgressions, He was bruised for our iniquities; the chastisement of our peace was upon Him; and with His stripes, we are healed". (Isaiah 53:5)

Jesus became our sin at the cross, so that by accepting Him as our Lord and Savior, we receive His *perfect test score* making us righteous, or *in right standing* with God for all of eternity.

"If He is willing to give you Christ, He is willing to freely give you every good thing." (Romans 8:32)

God is not a car-wrecking, cancer-causing Creator, but a loving Heavenly Father and He loves you as if you were the only person in this world to love! 2*

26

CHAPTER 4

What's in Your Backpack?

Up to this point we have covered how God created our spirit, soul, and body. Adam and Eve once were spiritually alive in all three parts but lost that innate connection to God when they entered disobedience. Jesus's sacrifice on the cross became our rescue story and the *only way* back to restoration of what we had lost. Let's now see the life changing benefit to our spirit, soul and body due to the price He paid reconnecting us to our heavenly Father.

Reestablishing that we are a spirit, we have a soul and live in a body is the basis for a solid understanding of how we were designed to operate in this world. Without this foundational truth, it is difficult to comprehend and fully appreciate just how special God made each of us.

You Have a Soul

You are a Spirit

You live In a Body

Thessalonians confirms we are made up of 3 distinct parts.

"And the very God of Peace sanctify you wholly; and I pray God your whole spirit, soul, and body be preserved blameless unto the coming of our Lord Jesus Christ." 1 Thessalonians 5:23

Your *Spiritual Backpack*

When Jesus paid the ultimate price by dying for our sins and taking our poverty, we in turn received His great riches, according to Luke 15. The Holy Spirit Himself came to take up residence in our spirit man, not our soul or body, to lead and guide those who accept Jesus. If it helps you to understand this concept, think of your spirit man being given a Holy Spirit spiritual backpack. Anyone who hikes or camps understands that it is essential to have the right things in your backpacks. It could mean the difference between living or dying if you are on a long journey away from home. Heaven is our real home; we are merely on a journey here until we finish and complete our race.

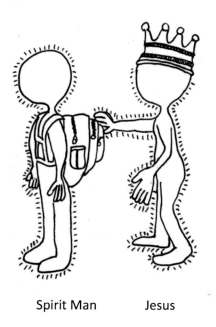

Spirit Man   Jesus

Our lives are not about trying to *get* from God; they are more about positioning ourselves to receive and release what He has already provided in our spiritual backpack. In football terms, the receiver needs to run the play that the quarterback calls and position himself to correct spot where the ball will be thrown. The Holy Spirit is our trusted quarterback and teacher giving us the correct play and showing us how to position ourselves to be receivers of what God has already provided. The football receiver runs by faith to the position. Therefore, it is important to know your position in Christ. "He will guide you unto all truth and show you things to come." (**John 16:13**)

Our backpack is full and complete! "According to His divine power *hath given unto us ALL THINGS* that pertain unto life and godliness through the knowledge of Him that hat called us to glory and virtue." (**2 Peter 1:3**)

All things means *all things*, but you cannot omit the knowledge part which is our responsibility to obtain. *Knowing* God's will is vital to *doing* God's will. What is God's will? God's will is His Word; The Bible. Is it possible to know God's will? Yes! Romans 12:2 answers this question:

"And be not conformed to this world: but be ye transformed by the renewing of your mind, that ye may prove what is that good, and acceptable, and perfect, will of God." (Romans 12:2)

The issue here is that you cannot believe beyond what you know. "Grace and peace be multiplied unto you through the knowledge of God, and of Jesus our Lord, According as his divine power hath given unto us all things that pertain unto life and godliness, through the knowledge of him that hath called us to glory and virtue." (**2 Peter 1:2-3**)

The only way to have more knowledge is to be taught more knowledge, but that requires some work. This means that we must labor into His rest. The more you time you spend with God in prayer or meditation, the more revealed knowledge you will have. Meditation here means giving your full attention to what God's Word is speaking to your mind. Worry would be an example of meditation on things **not** of God. We all know how to meditate, but the subject of the meditation can either bring joy, peace, and blessings, or steal those things from you.

What's in your Backpack?

How will you ever really know what Jesus paid for and made available in your spiritual backpack if you never explore God's Word. As you read this list of things that might be found in a survival backpack for a hiker, think about the similarities of what we have from Jesus in our Spiritual backpack.

Hydration   Living Water (John 7:38)

Tent/Sleeping Bag   Enlarge the place of your tent (Isaiah 54:2)

Knife   God's Word like a sword (Hebrews 4:12)

Fire Starter   Ideas to create (Proverbs 8:12)

Compass and Map   Holy Spirit direction (Psalm 143:10)

First aid kit   Healing (1 Peter 2:24)

Cooking equipment   Utensils for honorable work (2 Tim 2:20-21)

Change of clothes   Clean up and change your clothes (Gen 35:2)

Flashlight   God's Word to show you The Way (John 14:6)

Multi tool   God is our multi-faceted wisdom (Eph 3:10-12)

Cordage   Cord of three strands not easily broken (Eccl. 4:12)

Shovel   Thoroughly equipped to accomplish the job (2 Tim 3:17)

Knowing what resources are in your backpack is just as important as having them!

I have a good friend of mine who ministers primarily to college students and relies on a network of outside sources for his family's income. There was a point in time that contributions from his donors had dropped significantly and he was in need of two things: encouragement and money!

I sent to him a very nice Bible that had an extensive concordance built into it for reference and in my accompanying letter of encouragement, suggested that a very important scripture to read from this reference Bible would be Jeremiah 29:11. Since my friend was hungry for some financial answers from God, the best place to look first for answers is to learn what God has to say about finances in His Word and see what is available in our spiritual backpack.

Some time went by and one day I received a card in the mail thanking me for the reference Bible and the encouragement. It was obvious to me that he had not checked out the one specific scripture I had mentioned, or he would have found the large sum of money that I tightly tucked between the pages where Jeremiah 29:11 could be found. He may have thought, "Oh, I've read that scripture before, I know what it says without going there again." Do we really know what the verse means? It is not that God is going to insert money in a Bible to get you to read a verse, but the same verse you read a year ago can have new meaning now for your mind and your circumstances for today, because the Word is alive! It knows when you read it, what you need, and how to supply your needs! Our destiny requires our focus. Some people are more comfortable with the problem than desire the solution. God will never do *for you* what He delegated *to you*.

There are also Plans in Your Spiritual Backpack

 "For I know the plans I have for you," declares the Lord, "plans to prosper you and not harm you, plans to give you hope and a future. **(Jeremiah 29:11)**

This verse reflects a principle of God's grace over believers in Christ and his affections for those who He loves. He has made plans to give us hope for today and our future. Similarly, when we make plans for our own family and loved ones for their benefit after we are gone, it is called a will or living trust. These methods are a couple of the most important building blocks for estate planning. They allow you to lovingly put into words your best for those you have left behind.

These estate planning documents basically explain and clarify the specific details of what you want to happen with your property and assets once you are gone, and they will determine who will inherit, when they will inherit, and how they will inherit what you have left behind. To be enforced and become credible, the paperwork must be signed, witnessed, and notarized. Everyone becomes particularly interested in the will or living trust when someone dies because that is when the assets are distributed.

Jesus has a far better plan for us with a legacy of eternal blessings to pass along to us. His plan or will for us is called the "New Testament". "Testament" (covenant): "The last disposition which one makes of his earthly possessions after his death, a testament or will." (Thayer's Greek Lexicon).

His will describes for us in detail, His great love for us; it tells who will inherit, when and how we will inherit, and it is witnessed by God and the Holy Spirit.

"By the grace of God found in Jesus Christ our Savior, a person may become an heir of Christ.   (Titus3:5-7)

It was signed in Jesus's blood and notarized by the action of His death on the cross.

His will has a much greater reach than the ones that we use. Here is the contrast: Jesus's will benefits not only every person that has accepted Him as Lord and Savior after he died and paid the price for sin, but also reaches back to save those who believed in God before Jesus was born here on earth as a man.   Salvation always comes by grace through faith and not through works. An example of this is found in the Old Testament. In Genesis 15:6 it says, "And he (Abraham) believed in (had faith in) The Lord; and He (The Lord) counted it to him for righteousness." Abraham trusted God with the knowledge he had and is now in heaven!

Here is what Jesus Christ's will contains:

Romans 8:17 says that we are joint heirs with Jesus...not sub-heirs. What He owns, we now own. What He has, we have!

I John 4:16-17 says ...As He is, so are we in this world. (By the way, that means now.)

Look long and hard at this chart and begin to see yourself the way God sees you, joint heirs with Christ!

You Already Have It!

Luke 15:31-32 tells the story of the prodigal son who left his family, moved away, and spent all his money on things of the flesh, or worldly desires. After the son had spent all his inheritance, he finally hit rock bottom. As he was sitting with the pigs and about to have slop for dinner, something clicked in his thinking. The prodigal son came to the end of himself and was convicted of his sin and began thinking about how he would request forgiveness from his father. Here is the most beautiful part of the story:

"So he returned home to his father. And while he was still a long way off, his father saw him coming. Filled with love and compassion, he ran to his son, embraced him, and kissed him." (Luke 15:20)

His father saw him from a long way off, meaning he had been waiting with hopeful expectation. The next thing the son did was to tell the father that he had sinned and that he was not worthy to be called his son. It is important to see that *the father never condemned the son or wanted to talk about his past*. No, the father chose to celebrate and had servants give his son the best robe, put a ring on his finger and shoes on his feet. The father had every right to be mad but celebrated that although his son was once lost, now he was found! If you have ever had a situation where one of your children went missing, all your focus was on the one who was lost. What a moment of excitement when your child was found! God highly values lost things! This story is a parallel of who God is and how He operates. Is He waiting on you to return home to Him today?

The elder son heard all the celebration and came to the house from the fields to see what all the commotion was about and asked a servant. This made the elder son unhappy because he felt that he should have had all the things his returning brother was receiving. The father responded in this way:

"And he said unto him, Son, thou art ever with me, and *all that I have is thine*. It was meet that we should make merry and be glad: for this thy brother was dead, and is alive again; and was lost, and is found." (Luke 15:31,32)

"All that I have is thine." Many of us are praying for stuff that has already been given to us. The elder son had a problem with trying to become what he already was. He did not *feel* like his father loved him and would give what he asked for, so he never asked. Never let your feelings dictate your direction, choose your direction.

Like the father in this story, God's love is never based on the character of the receiver. God's love is based on the character of the Giver. *3 Trying to become something that you already are is the biggest source of Christian frustration. If you are saved, you are not only a child of God, but you are righteousness meaning a right standing with God, and able to receive *all things* that pertain to life and Godliness.

Chapter 5

What Changed When I Got Saved?

Thinking about my own salvation experience, I began to wonder whether it was it really my soul that got reborn and saved like I had always heard. So, if it was my soul that got saved, where do the spirit and body come in on this deal?

Reading and studying the Word, I began to ask the Lord about the differences in the spirit, soul, and body. I researched and found that there are 411 references in the bible to spirit, 437 references mentioning soul, and 678 references to the body. That is a lot to digest without help to understand. From the moment of being saved at the age of 12, I never heard a message regarding the real difference between the spirit, the soul, and the body. I attended a denominational church throughout much of my life and did not question the subject, assuming that the spirit and soul were really one. One day it occurred to me that I was not the only person who did not understand who I really was in Christ. Just as I used to assume, most people think that the spirit and the soul are really the same thing and have never understood that God made us a tri-part being.

You may ask, "Okay, why is it really important to understand the parts of my person? Is this one of those things in the Bible that will really matter to me now, or is it like studying the book of Revelation, which happens in the future? You know, I'm already saved and doing okay; how does understanding spirit, soul and body help me?"

Two reasons:

1) If you are already saved, the knowledge that you are a tri-part being will further accelerate your understanding of The Word and will help you improve all areas of your life. It gives you the missing puzzle pieces, revealing a clearer picture of just how special God made us and will enable you

to see so many more provisions for an abundant life. You will realize that it is not about trying to get God to move on your behalf, because He already has! It is about you learning how to receive what He has already provided for you in every area of your life! Finally, you will see how deep His love is for you because that is what removes all doubt so you may walk in faith.

2) If you are not saved yet, and you think that man is only a physical being created to satisfy his physical and emotional needs, you are losing sight of the fact that we are immortal. Understanding spirit, soul and body will help you realize that when God made you, He created a masterpiece. He is not mad at you but madly in love with you! This knowledge will help open your eyes to receive the most important gift you will ever know, Jesus Christ! You will understand that we are more than physical beings and that we do not cease to exist after dying. Just like a back-up generator for power at your home when the lights go off, an external generator comes roaring to life in you, and your spirit and soul will be transported to one of two places, when you die: heaven or hell.

The next couple of verses I read told me that by accepting Jesus as my savior, we are not only made new, but we are also made righteous! The message of (2 Corinthians 5:17-18) will be referred to several times, as it is foundational to understanding the truth that you are 100% righteous in your spirit man right now!

"Therefore, if any man be in Christ, he is a new creature: old things are passed away; behold, all things are become new. And all things of God, who hath reconciled us to himself by Jesus Christ." **(2 Corinthians 5:17-18)**

"For He had made Him to be sin for us, who knew no sin; that we might be made the righteousness of God in Him". (**2 Corinthians 5:21**)

This does not say that you will be a new creature sometime in the future; you are a new creature in your spirit man the instant that you are born again! However, this is not the case for the soul man and the body. The soul man is made up of your mind, your will, and your intellect just the same as before. You will think a lot of the same thoughts, and still have the same emotions. If you were overweight before you got saved, you will not instantly be the ideal weight or shape immediately after you are reborn because the change was in the spirit man, not the soul or the body. It is up to us to renew our minds (soul man) daily to the image of God placed inside of our spirit man which is His Glory!

I once wondered, "If I am a new creature and truly righteous, why do I still tend to sin? How can I have bad thoughts about things or people?" Then I found something interesting in Romans.

"And not only they but ourselves also, which have the first fruits of the spirit, even we ourselves groan within ourselves, waiting for the adoption, to wit the redemption of our body." (Romans 8:23)

When meditating on this verse, I began to understand that my spirit actually got saved and my soul and body are still *work in progress*. Romans 8:23 explains being 100% redeemed in our Spirit man is the first fruits of the spirit, and later comes the full redemption of our Soul and Body.

"And not only they, but ourselves also, which have the firstfruits of the Spirit, even we ourselves groan within ourselves, waiting for the adoption, to wit, the redemption of the body." (Romans 8:23)

Look at the word "adoption" for a moment. Just as when children are adopted, there is a process to become part of God's Family. The process of our adoption begins with our decision to join God's Family. Why would you want to join God's family? God loves you so much that He does not want you to perish. Jesus Christ is the only antidote for sin, and you must have it by accepting Him before your physical death.

Adam and Eve were created by God to live forever, but when they violated God's law of sin and death, they paid the consequence. Violating a physical law such as gravity could be compared to violating a spiritual law like God's law of sin and death found in Romans 8:1-2.

"There is therefore now no condemnation to them which are in Christ Jesus, who walk not after the flesh, but after the Spirit. For the law of the Spirit of life in Christ Jesus hath made me free from the law of sin and death." (Romans 8:1-2)

Disagreeing with or ignoring the law of gravity or God's spiritual laws does not change the fact that they are real, and both have repercussions. God commanded to Adam in Genesis 2:17 to not eat from the tree of good and evil "for in the day you eat of it you shall surely die." Adam and Eve violated God's law of sin and death, and we as their descendants are still experiencing the effects.

As we age, the skin wrinkles, hair grays, and sight weakens. This is not because we are sick, but because death is operating in us. It is a progression that starts with the body. Since the body is our legal right to exist on this earth, the moment it dies, your soul man and your spirit must leave for one of two destinations. In Christ Jesus there is a law that lifts you up, just as in the natural there is a law of death that pulls you down. Christianity and salvation are the conscious taking of yourself out of the law of death and putting yourself into the conscious control of the law of life. "The law of the Spirit of life in Christ Jesus hath made me free of the Law of sin and death." (Romans 8:2)

Let me explain this more fully...

When we accept Jesus as our Savior and experience a rebirth, our spirit man awakens and becomes 100% redeemed. God's Holy Spirit comes to reside in our spirit man once again, just as in the spirits of Adam and Eve before the fall, we become one-third renewed. Our spirit man gets perfectly sealed by the Holy Spirit and made 100% perfect.

Someone told you about Jesus and you believed. At this point a down payment was made on your eternal inheritance.

"In whom you also trusted after that you heard The Word of Truth the Gospel of your salvation, in who also after you believed, you were "Sealed" with that Holy Spirit of Promise which is the earnest of your inheritance until the redemption of the purchased possession unto the praise of His Glory". (Ephesians 1:13-14)

What is the promise Ephesians is talking about? After you heard about Jesus and made Him the Lord of your life, He took your sins, and you received His righteousness. Jesus got your rags, and you got His riches. Your spirit man became 100% righteous and you became one-third redeemed. This was the earnest money, or down payment for a part of your inheritance until full redemption day. As you understand righteousness more fully, you become more conscious of righteousness than the sin and condemnation that come from living in the flesh.

When is full redemption day? This day occurs when Jesus comes back again to receive all who have made Him Lord of their lives in what is referred to as the Rapture or *catching away of the church*. At that time, we will receive the rest of our inheritance and we will not only be 100% righteous in our spirits, but also in our soul and our bodies.

"Behold, I show you a mystery; We shall not all sleep, but we shall all be changed,
In a moment, in the twinkling of an eye, at the last trump: for the trumpet shall sound, and the dead shall be raised incorruptible, and we shall be changed. (1 Corinthians 15:51-52)

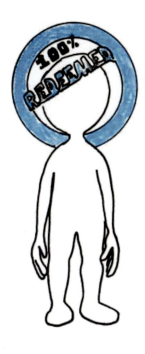 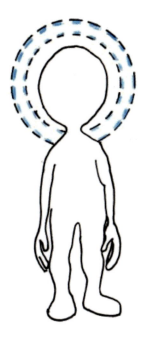 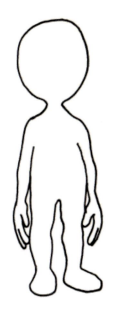

First fruits of **The Spirit**	**Soul**	**Body**
God in us now, is the down payment	Work in progress	Whole construction site

God's glory and righteousness were imparted to Adam's spirit, soul and body but lost in the garden of Eden, are now fully restored to man's spirit. When we accept Jesus as our Lord and Savior, our spirit man, rather than our soul man got reborn. We are now restored to a position of authority in our spirit man and the Holy Spirit takes up residence there to be our constant guide throughout our days here on the earth and eternity! Our spirit man needs no maintenance with God living on the inside of us.

**Your spirit man got reborn
when you accepted Jesus!**

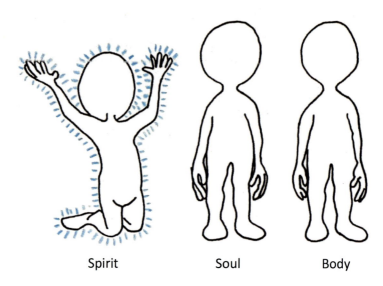

| Spirit | Soul | Body |

As the soul man and body are not fully restored, we still find ourselves with the need to work on these areas. Therefore, we are told to renew our minds to God's Word. There are a couple of verses that help explain this more about the state of the body as the outward man and the soul as being the inward man.

"For which cause we faint not, but though our outward man perish, yet the inward man is renewed day by day. (II Corinthians 4:16)

In 1 John 4:17 we see that "As Jesus is, so are we in this world."

Now after reading these verses, it becomes clear how we could be made righteous in our spirit man now, not later. Notice the phrase *in this world* in 1 John 4:17. It does not say later in Heaven. It reads that we are righteous now *here on earth in this world,* and have the same legal authority that Jesus has over the devil. That is worth shouting about!

We do not *become* righteous; we are *made* righteous. Just as sin came through one man, Adam, it is also true that through one man, Jesus Christ, forgiveness was made available for our sin. Now we have gifts of grace and righteousness that we receive through faith. Grace here is defined as not giving to us what we deserve; and righteousness as putting us into a right standing again with God.

Righteousness is the ability to stand in the presence of God without a sense of guilt, condemnation, or inferiority. It is much easier to live in righteousness if you understand that you are already righteous. God is in the business of convicting us of sin to help us turn away from it, while satan is in the business of condemning us for our sin and leaving us with the impression that there is no way out. Once we receive our salvation, the mind of Christ and the wisdom of God are inside us. Where? In our spirit man! The wisdom of God was set aside for those who accept Him for our glory.

"But my God will supply all your needs according to His riches in glory by Christ Jesus. **(Philippians 4:19)**

Where is Jesus? He is inside of your spirit man in the form of the Holy Spirit.

"Therefore, if any man be in Christ, he is a *new creature*: old things are passed away; behold all things are become new." (II Cor 5:17-18)

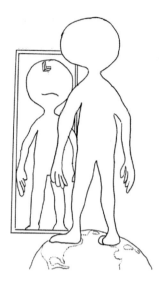

When you look at yourself in the mirror and reflect in your mind about your personality and appearance, who do you see? Do you see someone who is imperfect and lacking in several areas, or someone who is confident and complete in Christ Jesus? If we are looking at our souls and bodies it is understandable why we might see ourselves that way, because we are not made perfect in these two areas...yet.

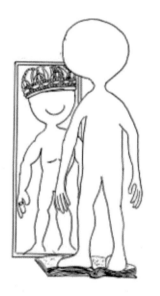

However, if you are a born-again child of God you are a **new creation** in your spirit man and you are made in perfect righteousness with nothing missing and nothing broken. When we become *born again*, the Spirit of God (meaning The Holy Spirit), enters into our spirit man (1 John 4:13) and begins to communicate/relate with our spirit (Romans 8:15-16)

"Hereby know we that we dwell in him, and he in us, because he hath given us of His Spirit." (1 John 4:13)

"For ye have not received the spirit of bondage again to fear; but ye have received the Spirit of adoption, whereby we cry, Abba, Father. The Spirit itself beareth witness with our spirit, that we are the children of God." (Romans 8:15-16)

Accepting Jesus as your Lord and Savior is the point of your new birth and the Holy Spirit comes and takes up residence to live inside your spirit man. Now instead of God just being *with you* like the saints in the Old Testament experienced at times, you now have God *in you*! You no longer must pray, "God, please be with us" because He says that He will never leave nor abandon you.

"...for he hath said, I will never leave thee, nor forsake thee."
(Hebrews 13:5)

Under the old covenant, angels were the messengers of communication to man because Jesus had not paid the price for our sins so that the Holy Spirit could come and live on the inside of our spirit man. God could not reveal himself to natural man, but angels could be seen and heard to deliver news. However, in the new covenant, Paul had the Holy Spirit living on the inside of his spirit man. He was able to hear from God in his spirit man and received revelation about Jesus. This revealed knowledge in Paul's spirit enabled him to write two thirds of the New Testament. No angel had to bring him this revelation.

The good news is this that from now on when God looks at us, He sees us in our perfect born-again spirit complete in Christ in every way! You see, you are not in crisis...you are in Christ!

Some people receive their salvation and accept Jesus as their Savior but refuse to grow up spiritually; they never develop their spirits and souls to understand the riches that God has provided to them. We see an example of this in **Job 32:7-8**. "I said days should speak, and multitude of years should teach wisdom. But there is a spirit in man: and the inspiration of the Almighty giveth understanding." People think that a long life of days should produce wisdom, but sometimes age arrives all by itself. You might say their souls are undeveloped because they do not spend enough time in the Word or with Him in prayer. Think of your Bible as a spiritual mirror that reflects an image of who you really are in Christ.

God's Word is our spiritual mirror

In other words, the Word of God describes to you how our Creator sees us. God looks at us in our born-again spirits! This is the truth of our identities; and 2 Corinthians describes the real you!

"Therefore, if anyone is in Christ, he is a new creation. The old has gone, the new has come." (2 Corinthians 5:17)

If our focus is on who we are in our bodies, then we are susceptible to feelings of condemnation and inferiority, yet God sees us in our spirit man which is already complete in Christ and lacking no good thing. You do not just become better; you are a brand-new creation in your spirt man!

Let's look at the spirit, soul and body hierarchy, in reverse. All of us know who we are in body because we are constantly using our five senses to interpret only physical things.

Body Interprets physical things only by:

- Sight
- Hearing
- Smell
- Taste
- Touch

Our soul man interprets spiritual and physical things and is comprised of our mind, will and emotions. Think of your soul man as housing the *thinker*, the *chooser,* and the *feeler*. Unfortunately, the natural tendency is to allow our will to side with our emotions first. This is our default mode with not much balance from the mind. God gave us emotions and they represent an especially important part of who we are. The important thing to remember is that we must use wisdom to keep our emotions in check because it is the reaction, not the emotion that causes trouble. "A fool expresses all his emotions, but a wise person controls them. **(Proverbs 29:11)**

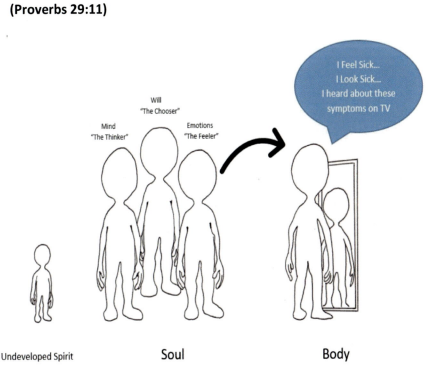

We have our will to be the chooser or tiebreaker between our emotions and reason. If you have never made the decision to receive Jesus as you Lord and Savior, you have an undeveloped Spirit Man.

All the information that comes into your body goes directly to your physical brain. Your brain is the processing and storage center for daily experiences and interactions from the day that you are born. In technological terms, you could compare your physical brain to a server. A server is a computer with a software program which manages and gives order to information or data received. It has RAM or (random access memory) of the stored information for recall to be used or shared with other servers.

As we learned in school, for every physical input our body receives there is a corresponding voluntary or involuntary response. A reflex action is an involuntary response, and results in action without thinking. When an action includes the involvement of thoughts, it is called voluntary. It stands to reason, that we should always involve our mind before our will makes the choice. Anything less means we are living by our emotions.

Your Soul is the processing center for spiritual and physical things. III John 2 says your soul prospers when you feed your spirit on God's Word. If you are not saved, your spirit man is undeveloped and there is limited input from the wisdom of God to reveal deeper truths to your spirit and soul. Therefore, you will find yourself relying on your physical senses.

There have been many successful people in this world who made it through trusting their physical senses and copying things that worked for others, but in the end where is the real value in that method? **Mark 8:36 asks**, "For what profits a man if he gains the whole world but loses his own soul?" A life separated from God focuses on an earth-bound perspectives and ambitions. What good is it for someone to have climbed the ladder of earthly success, only to realize toward the end of their life that it was leaned up against the wrong wall? In other words, life involves more than what you have attained that will soon be forgotten, but what you have given to God which is eternal.

CHAPTER 6

Follow-the-Leader

The Alcan (Alaska-Canada) highway was built during World War II to connect Alaska with the lower forty-eight states.   Stretches of this gravel road were rough and muddy from melted winter, which meant that severe ruts formed when things froze over again. Back in the 1960s before it was paved, there was a sign upon entering Alaska that reads: "Choose your rut carefully — you will be in it for the next 200 miles." Just as the ruts on the Alcan Highway were predictable, so are our problems when our souls choose paths that align with our bodies instead of our spirits. Your body may currently be your default leader, but your flesh and emotions were never meant to be the leaders of your life.

Who's Your Leader?

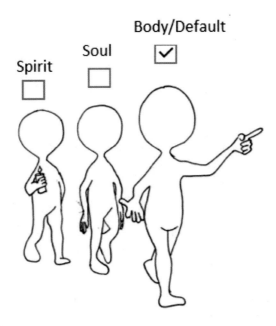

The children's game of follow-the-leader is played by first choosing a leader, then the remaining children line up behind. All the followers must follow the same path and mimic the leader's actions to stay in the game. The important lesson for us here is to recognize whom we have selected as our leader, and what outcome we can expect. Our decisions and actions are not independent of each other. Paths taken in life tend to have predictable outcomes. Life is connected, and even the friends we choose will be a determining factor of outcomes we will experience. Often people will choose to do what others do simply because of the fear of embarrassment of fear of being wrong. Herd mentality is not always bad, but when following and adhering to a particular herd with selfish objectives and void of truth, you should run the other way!

The good news is that as born-again believers, we have the benefit of being led by the Spirit of God. It is your spirit man that should be leading because it is the real you and the one that relates to God, not our bodies. We are to control our mind and senses from our spirit man. When this occurs, the character and choices that we express outwardly reflect those of the Holy Spirit living on the inside of our spirit. Since God knows the end from the beginning, His wisdom will help you make better decisions not just based on hindsight, but also foresight. **John 16:13** says it like this:

"But when He, the Spirit of Truth, comes, He will guide you into all truth. He will not speak on His own; He will speak only what He hears, and He will tell you what is yet to come."

We are not following the right leader when we are primarily led by the body, we are following our fleshly desires. When our spirit is led by the Holy Spirit, we draw from God first to fulfill our real needs, so that we do not become totally dependent on trying to draw from another man's well. From the Holy Spirit we find peace and emotional stability instead of neediness.

We use our ears and to draw from Jesus; we use our hands and feet (words and deeds) to serve Him. "And whatever you do in word and deed, do it all in the Name of Jesus." (**Colossians 3:17**) When we try to draw from each other only what God can supply, we will be unfulfilled: un - full - filled. This is the main reason for the broken relationships we may have as well as failed marriages.

If you throw a rock into a pack of dogs, the one that barks is the one that got hit. Likewise, the person who still feels injured from a previous relationship may choose to drag that offense into a new relationship with you and will make you pay for what someone else did to them.

We must recognize that God gave us free will and, that we can actually choose the attitudes we presently have. Operating from your spirit and soul rather than from your soul and body is the way live at peace with one another. This directs you to first draw from God, so you may fulfill (fully fill) each other.

How do you know if you are operating in your born-again spirit or your soul? Ask yourself these simple questions:

- Are you basically the same positive, stable person all the time?
- Do you live based on how you feel emotionally or physically in the moment?
- Do situations rock your world??
- Do you have patience with people or things?
- Do you lead to be somebody, or lead to help somebody?
- Are you jealous of other's success or are you encouraging?
- Do you genuinely love others, and especially the unlovely?

If you are not the same all the time, you are not walking in the spirit which means that you are living in the default mode of soul and body. If you are in Christ and live knowing that you are in Christ, then you are allowing the real you to come through your soul man. Once your soul bears witness or agrees with your spirit man, a majority rule occurs. It is two against one! In doing so, your responses to adversity, rejection, and condemnation do not bring you down because you are not focused on yourself, but others. It would be natural for us to feel deprived if we are only thinking about ourselves.

Spirit	Soul	Body

Matthew 18:19 says "If two of you shall agree on earth as touching anything that they ask, it shall be done for them of my Father which is in heaven." We have usually understood this to mean that if two believers agree according to a promise in God's Word it would be done. But what about your spirit and soul standing in agreement to effect one of God's promises? **II Corinthians 13:1** would confirm that "In the mouth of two or three witnesses shall every word be established."

Say you make plans with a friend to meet for dinner at a specific restaurant and time on Friday. Throughout the day it seems that one obstacle after another comes at you trying to steal your joy. Finally, the end of a frustrating day comes, and you get in your car to leave work. Only as you are about to pull into your neighborhood do you remember your friend and dinner plans. Since it is now 30 minutes past the agreed time, you rush to call your friend and apologize. They too had a busy day and have become totally frustrated because you inconvenienced them. Words are exchanged and what would have been a great dinner has turned into hurt feelings.

Walking in Christ or (in the spirit) means that we do not take offense to the shortcomings of others. Life happens, and when we are walking by our feelings or (in the flesh), we are more prone to get angry because our focus is on ourselves.

When you can step back while all of this is happening and see that we are operating out of our feelings rather than in our spirit man, you can bring your emotions back into line with something immensely powerful called a decision. Decide to have a long fuse. Yes, you can adhere to the advice in *Psalms* and refuse to be offended. This could diffuse the entire situation and maybe even save a friendship. "Great peace have they which love thy law; and nothing shall offend them." **(Psalm 119:165)**

Do You Care More About What Others Think Than What God Thinks?

Puberty brings about its own set of challenges with a changing body, but there are changes in our souls as well. We can become more preoccupied with feelings and the opinions of our peers. Not knowing who you are in Christ takes you down a path of walking in the flesh. In other words, you are more in tune with your feelings and emotions that come from the opinions of others than the opinion of God. Do you care more about what others think and say about you than what God thinks and says about you? Please understand, you will never find peace in another person's head. It is nice to be liked by others you deem important, but it is far more important to understand you are loved by our Creator first. Others will fail you, but He never will.

Living by your feelings is like never uncrating your recreated spirit man.

When there is limited knowledge about your reborn spirit man, you may live your life void of its wisdom and influence. The consequence of lacking knowledge will propel you to live by your feelings and emotions. There are two kinds of faith: natural faith and spiritual faith. Natural faith comes from natural birth and relies on your five physical senses. Spiritual faith comes from God (Ephesians 2:8) and comes from Him. "For by grace are ye saved through faith; and that of yourselves; it is the gift of God."

Status

I heard many years ago that the definition of status is trying to impress someone you do not like with something you usually cannot afford. If we never find out who we are in Christ when we are younger, as we turn into grown adults, the problem manifests itself in a never-ending struggle of trying to impress others with stuff or position. Boiling it all down, it is pride.

Today social media gives us the opportunity to present the best side of our lives to others. When we see the excitement and success of others and focus on how we feel rather than on being happy for them, it can trigger discouragement and depression. If we are being led by your emotions, we may try to even the field in our minds by posting more about our own successes on Facebook. We should always care more what our Heavenly Father thinks about us than what others think. He has something more important called *Faithbook*!

Allowing our emotions to be in the driver's seat can cause stress, anxiety, and disappointment. It causes us to focus on what we do not have, rather than on being thankful for what we do have. In Genesis, Adam and Eve had it all, except that one tree that God directly instructed Adam not to eat from. The devil always pinpoints that one thing in our lives that we do not have to cause us disappointment and poor judgment.

Being Double-Minded or Finding Real Truth

Did you know that you could be double minded? If you are double-minded, you are flying in and out of the spirit, soul, and body.

Spirit   Soul   Body

Double-Mindedness explained:

"A double-minded man is unstable in all his ways." (James 1:8) He hears the voice of his conscience (spirit man) but allows his carnal passions to override his decision making.

Our daily decisions determine our direction. Our direction determines our destiny. For those who are not renewing their minds to the Word on a regular basis, disagreement between their spirit, soul and body is inevitable. If our decisions are based on our feelings rather than truths, they are void of wisdom. Operating in life without a true north will make all other degrees of direction in your life inaccurate.

A compass can direct you to a magnetic north which is a point located in the Artic region of Canada. (I know this is probably a little too much detail for most of you, but for my engineers, accountants, and analytical friends who like specifics, here you go!) In addition to a magnetic north there is something called true north. Think of the earth or our world as having a large bar magnet on the inside, but the problem is that the world's magnet is not perfectly aligned with the *truth* or *true* North and South Poles. This means that if you were to use a magnetic compass that relies on the natural magnet of the world to find your way, you will not end up at the exact location you wanted. This could be compared to relying on your feelings to make decisions instead of truth.

People do not see life as it is, they see life as they are. The frame we put around our life might not be truth, but it is how we see it. A person's worldview is formed from both physical and emotional experiences from birth until the present. Just because the compass may point to a magnetic north, or because you feel a certain way, that does not necessarily mean you are interpreting directions accurately.

God deals in truth all the time. **(John 4:24)** says, "God is Spirit, and they that worship Him must worship Him in spirit and truth." Turning to God's Word brings our spirit, soul, and body into perfect alignment; it is the master key to all that is good!

The other factor that can cause issues in understanding truth are your past conclusions from experiences and other people's opinions that were not truth-based. Peer pressure, whether realized or not, influence the way we see things and places filters before our eyes.

Is your joy based on what is happening at the time or on who you are in Christ? Many live in the soul man, where happiness is from a *happening*. Real joy is an inside condition from your spirit man. This joy is fed directly from God, so you are not constantly chasing temporary outside things to make you happy, which are always short lived.

If you were ever abused growing up whether physically or emotionally think about this for a moment. What are the only ways you can be abused in this world? Physically? Emotionally?

Where does this abuse occur?

Physically – In the body / Pain is a signal there is a problem here.

Emotionally - In the soul / Doubt is a signal there is a problem here.

Where can no one abuse you?

Spiritually - In your spirit

Your spirit man is your refuge where God lives. Why not retreat there?

Whose Report Will You Believe?

Isaiah 53:1 "Who has believed our report? and to whom is the arm of the Lord revealed?

What this is really asking is, "Are you going to put faith in God, or in what you see in the natural?" Another way of explaining this is, "Will you listen to your spirit or your body in making decisions?"

Joshua and Caleb chose to believe God in Numbers 13 - 14 where we read the account of the twelve spies exploring Canaan, the Promised land. Joshua and Caleb saw with *spiritual eyes* and others with *physical eyes*.

Before the Israelites entered Canaan, the people requested that Moses send a spy into the land to scout it out and bring back a report. God confirmed it was His will for Moses to send a leader from each of the twelve tribes on a reconnaissance mission into Canaan to bring back a report. God's intentions for this mission were to better equip the Israelites to do battle in the land, and understand what the benefits were for conquering it by discovering the following:

- Whether the people who lived there were strong or weak
- Whether the land was good or bad

- Whether the cities were like camps or strongholds
- Whether the land was rich or poor
- Whether or not there were forests or wood there

The twelve spies did as Moses instructed and came back with reports on Canaan finding it to be a land flowing with milk and honey. However, ten of the spies were fearful and included a negative report that the inhabitants of the land were giants and the cities well-fortified which would discourage any battle. Only two spies, Caleb and Joshua trusted that God would enable Israel to take the land. (Numbers 14:6-9) In any battle or situation, we need to find out what God is saying first and believe His report.

Our problem is not in believing, because everyone believes something. The challenge is knowing *what* to believe. We have the choice to believe what the problem says or what God says. God's word planted in your heart yields belief, but belief is only harvested with corresponding action.

As a result of believing the wrong report, the Israelites were judged by God and made to wait 40 years to enter the land they were promised. Every person 20 years old and above would die in the wilderness never to ever see the land except Caleb and Joshua. They both had a different spirit, knowing what to believe and followed God. After Moses died 40 years later, Joshua led the Israelites across the Jordan River into the Promised Land because he chose life.

Choose Life

God wants us to choose life in every situation so that it goes well with us. **Deuteronomy 30:19** says, "I call heaven and earth to record this day against you, (that) I have set before you life and death, blessing and cursing: therefore, choose life, that both thou and thy seed may live." This verse came from Moses's pep talk to the Israelites before they were to cross the Jordan into the Promised Land. To boil it all down, he was basically saying, choose today what you will be happy with tomorrow. The first step is to realize that you have the power to decide.

CHAPTER 7

Knowing Who You Are

"For God so loved the world that He gave His only begotten Son, that whoever believes in Him should not perish, but have everlasting life." **(John 3:16)**. Since God has come down to earth and provided a plan for the mistake that Adam made in the garden through the birth, burial and resurrection of His son Jesus, where is He now? A lot of people question that, but the answer to this important question is found in His Word.

Jesus said to him, "I am the way, the truth, and the life. No one comes to the Father except through me." **(John 14:6)**

There is only one way to God and that is through his precious son Jesus. Like a popular album that was released called *Look up Child*, God is wanting us to simply look up to Him as a small child would. When we do not have everything in our lives nailed down or figured out, and it seems like we are in the middle of a battle, the simple action of looking up to Him is powerful.

When we do look up to God and ask, "Where are you now?", what comes to your mind? Do you think that He has left you because something bad has happened in your life? Does this cause you to doubt and wonder if He even cares about you or your problems? The good news is that God does care, and He is with us. "…. for he hath said, I will never leave thee, nor forsake thee." **(Hebrews 13:5)**

Most of us do not know who we are in Christ or even what that phrase means though you may have heard it all your life. The following explanation will help you demystify that part of who you are. When you know who you really are you will think differently, which means that you will act and communicate differently.

Benefits of understanding who you are in Christ

"He said to them, 'But who do you say that I am?' Peter answered and said to Him, 'You are the Christ.'" **(Mark 8:29)**

How you see Jesus determines how you see yourself. Jesus paid the price not only for our salvation so that we may become born again (which starts in our Spirit Man), but also for the other things we need while we are on this earthly journey as ambassadors for Jesus. Paul writes that we are Christ's ambassadors. **(2 Corinthians 5:20)**. The Greek word for ambassador is *presbeuo*, and it shares the same root word as presbyter, which also means church leader. Although we may not be leaders in the churches we attend, we are all ambassadors of Christ with the mission of representing Jesus to this world.

The main reason you might have a challenge accepting this fact is that you may not fully know who you are in Christ regarding this aspect of our place here on earth. The New Testament tells us how: "God made him [Jesus] who had no sin to be sin for us, so that in him we might become the righteousness of God" **(2 Corinthians 5:21)**. When God sees you as a born-again child of His, He sees your righteousness or Jesus in you. That is because your spirit man was born again and 100% redeemed to be like Jesus. Your soul man and your body are not yet redeemed, and our default understanding of many things in life is physical in nature. As a result, many times we do not see things from the perspective of how God sees us, being that He is looking squarely at our born again re-created spirit.

The people in the hometown where Jesus grew up saw him in the natural. They looked with physical eyes and Nathaniel said, "Can anything good come out of Nazareth?" **(John 1:45-46)**

Matthew tells a similar story. "Therefore, they said of Him, 'is this not the carpenter's son? Is not His mother called Mary? And His brothers James, Joses, Simon, and Judas? And his sisters, are they not all with us?'" **(Matthew 13:55-56)**

Since they saw Him in only His earth suit and looked at his natural family, He did not do many mighty works there. (Matthew 13:58) Jesus came to be our righteousness or right standing before God. It is what I like to call the great exchange! He took our rags and gave us His riches in every area of our lives.

"But God demonstrates His own love toward us, in that while we were still sinners, Christ died for us." **(Romans 5:8)** When Jesus hung on the cross, he literally became sin for us. He became sickness, disease, lack, and poverty, so we would not have to endure these things. Christ has redeemed us from the curse of the law." (Gal 3:13,14) In Isaiah 53:5, we see how this this redemption specifically affected our spirit, soul and body individually. Check this out!

- (*Redemption of our spirit man*) - *But he was wounded for our transgressions, He was bruised for our iniquities*
- (*Redemption for our soul*) - the chastisement of our peace was upon Him
- (*Redemption for our body*) - ...and with His stripes we are healed

(Isaiah 53:5)

After redeeming our spirt, soul and body, Paul summed it up for us; we are righteous!

"For He hath made Him to be sin for us, who knew no sin that we might be made the righteousness (Right standing) with God through Him!" **(2 Cor 5:21)**

Romans 8:32 says that if He is willing to give you Christ, He is willing to freely give you *every good thing*.

Who Do You Say I AM?

Jesus asked his disciples once, "But who do you say that I am?" **(Matthew 16:15)** How you personally understand and answer this particularly important question is the basis for how you can see your own self as being righteous or not. After being born again, the Holy Spirit comes to live on the inside of our spirit, and we are made righteous. "Love had been perfected among us in this: that we may have boldness in the day of judgment; because as He is so are we in this world." **(1 John 4:17)** This must be our attitude.

We are sharing His life in our Spirit man now. As Jesus is in His health, so are we in this world; As Jesus is in His righteousness, so are we in this world. Our default image is usually only what our five senses pick up in this physical world. If we are not renewing our minds (soul man) to God's Word, we are hampering the blessings He wants to give us. A glass mirror is what we use to look at to see our physical body; the Bible is our mirror to see into our spirit man.

However, most Christians only see themselves in a physical mirror and not through God's eyes revealed to us by His Holy Spirit and His Word. You can never believe beyond your knowledge! If you never read the Bible, all you will ever know is what someone tells you. Readers are leaders! Check it out in **(II Peter 1:2-3)**: "Grace and peace be multiplied unto you through the knowledge of God, and of Jesus our Lord, According as his divine power hath given unto us all things that pertain unto life and godliness, through the knowledge of him that hath called us to glory and virtue". These verses should excite us because they show that there are gospel benefits when we read and have knowledge about who we are in our spirit man.

Simply put, we can figure things out how to be successful in *every area of our lives* when we see ourselves the way God sees us. How does God see us? Let me ask you a question…How do you see your small child who is struggling to tie his own shoes? Do you see him in adult life as walking around in flip flops because he never learned to tie his shoes? No way, you see the oak tree, not the acorn! That is exactly how God sees you! He sees the end from the beginning, which we cannot know precisely now, but we can rest assured that it is good! We are conditioned in this physical world to only live by what we see in front of our own eyes. We only see the float in front of us, but God sees the whole parade.

Remember Jeremiah 29:11?

"'For I know the plans I have for you,' declares The Lord, 'plans to prosper you and not harm you, plans to give you hope and a future.'" **(Jeremiah 29:11)**

With Facebook, we now have a tool to promote not only how we want to see ourselves, but also how we want others to view us. This social media platform, along with Instagram and Snapchat, gives us ready access to a vast audience and allows self-promotion to the extreme. Now, a <u>study</u> in the *Journal of Social and Clinical Psychology* *2 finds that not only do Facebook and depressive symptoms go hand-in-hand, but the mediating factor seems to be a well-established psychological phenomenon: social comparison. That is, making comparisons, often between our most humdrum moments and our friends' highlight reels – the vacation montages and cute baby pics – is what links Facebook time and depressive symptoms together. God created you to be a great original, do not die a cheap copy. 2 Corinthians warns that it is not wise for us to compare ourselves with others.

"For we dare not make ourselves of the number, or compare ourselves with some that commend themselves: but they measuring themselves by themselves, and comparing themselves among themselves, are not wise. (2 Corinthians 10:12)

Many of us enjoy scrolling through social media and seeing updates from family and friends, only to have our feeds interrupted by posts of people whom psychologists would describe as narcissists. They lean toward a view of themselves as being successful, prosperous, and exceptional. They promote their physical sides, therefore putting forth a façade of how they want people to view them. By posting views of only their best sides, narcissists can cultivate personas for the purpose of bringing even more attention to themselves.

What we really need to do is cultivate the image of who we are in Christ and adjust our attitudes about Facebook. When the party is over and all the friends are gone, God is still there. This quote is worth repeating: "There will come a day when all you have left is what you have given to God." *3 Pause for a moment and let it penetrate your thinking. All the physical things we are chasing are mentioned in Ecclesiastes, where the theme is "Here is what I have discovered about life."

I have seen all the works that are done under the sun; and, behold, all is vanity and vexation of spirit. That which is crooked cannot be made straight: and that which is wanting cannot be numbered. I communed with mine own heart, saying, Lo, I am come to great estate, and have gotten more wisdom than all they that have been before me in Jerusalem: yea, my heart had great experience of wisdom and knowledge. And I gave my heart to know wisdom, and to know madness and folly: I perceived that this also is vexation of spirit. **(Ecclesiastes 1:14-17)**

Vexation is like *feeding on the wind.* This phrase means people are wasting their lives feeding on things that really have no eternal benefit. There is nothing there and your hunger is never satisfied. The sad thing is, if you are focused on who you are in your body or soul, you will be blinded to what is happening. The result of focusing on who you are in your body and soul rather than who you are in your spirit man or in Christ, is that you are left with an emptiness and a wanting.

When you accepted Jesus as your Savior, you were made righteous by your position and not your performance. Righteousness is not *right doing* but *right standing* before God because you accepted Jesus. Jesus took your rags and gave you His riches so we must not keep trying to satisfy an already satisfied God! When you become legalistic and see things only through the lens of your soul and body, you will wind up having a firm grip on an empty bag. However, seeing life through your spirit man by the basic understanding of spirit, soul, and body will allow you to start living your life to the fullest and begin investing in things that have eternal substance and outcomes.

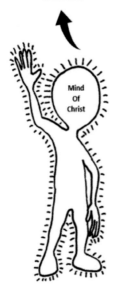

Searches the Spirit of God or things not seen.

The Tiebreaker

Searches the World and what it can see.

Mind Of Christ

Mind Of Man

Brain Info. Storage

Re-born Spirit
- The Real You!
- Contains God's DNA
- Heaven Ready
- Your Core Being

Soul
- Will
- Mind
- Intellect
- Emotions

Body
- Earth suit
- Permit to legally operate on this earth
- A physical copy of Your Spirit

When you understand that the salvation experience happens in the spirit man, it is easier to understand just what you need to do to experience this "glory" over in your soul and body. This glory on the inside of your spirit man after being saved is a result of the Holy Spirit that has taken up residence there.

"That the God of our Lord Jesus Christ, the Father of Glory, may give you the spirit of wisdom and revelation in the knowledge of Him. The eyes of your understanding being enlightened; that you may know what the hope of His calling is, and what the riches of the glory of His inheritance in the saints." **(Ephesians 1:17-18)**

These verses are telling us that you would know the hope of His calling, which is *the hope of His glory*. Pray that you will understand the riches of the glory of His inheritance in the saints. When we inherited Him, glory was deposited in our spirit man, but we must receive revelation of what it means to walk in that glory (or walk in the Spirit).

When we get genuinely saved, the change occurs in our spirit man. Our spirit man was reborn now having the mind of Christ and searches the things of God. The core of who we were in our spirit man changed in a big way, but we still have two parts that did not: our soul man and body. Therefore, if someone had a drinking problem before, it is a good probability that this issue will start to lose its control to dominate them because their spirit man now has a vote in the decision. If there was an addiction to smoking or eating, they may not necessarily lose that desire immediately because their mind (soul) must be renewed to the mind of Christ that now resides in their spirit man. Renewing our minds daily to God's Word will cause negative thoughts, addictions, poor habits, and the things of this world will grow dimmer while the things of God will grow stronger in our soul man.

But what you did sense, was an excitement on the inside. But where on the inside? In your heart? Do you mean the blood pump? Of course, not in your physical heart directly, because that is only the blood pump of your body that keeps us alive. It first occurred in the heart of your spirit man which excited the heart of your soul man (which is your mind, will and emotions), and eventually could influence the heart of your body, which could cause it to beat a little faster.

We receive this salvation so simply, but when we examine just what happened, not everyone can adequately put it into words. The main point is that you were saved by grace, (God giving you something that you did not earn) through faith in Jesus. You believed, confessed, and received Jesus as your Lord and Savior, and the Holy Spirit came into you or more specifically into your spirit man. Your spirit man became re-born and you became a new person. I once heard someone explain that "you got to get this understanding down in your knower." Well, that is a great way to put it, but this brings us to the next question, what exactly is our knower?

What is the Heart of Man?

This a great place to pause
and go a little deeper with
understanding the three
parts we just covered that
make up our *real identity*.
My longest standing question
when I first started
discovering the difference
between my spirit, soul and
body was about the word
heart.

Sometimes our culture uses
the same word to describe many things that have different levels of
importance. One such word is the word love. We use it all the time
for various purposes. People may commonly say "I love my car," or
"I love to go fishing." Although we generally understand what they
mean, when they say, "I love my wife," or "I love my children," does
this put family on the same platform of importance as their car or
something they do? When we use a word like love for so many
different feelings, it may get a little watered down or have quite
different meanings. The word I would like for us to focus on here
for a moment is heart.

The word heart is used to convey a thought about the core of
something and could represent several different things to us. When
we talk about the heart of an issue, we mean the most important
part. When we talk about driving through the heart of a city, we
mean the innermost or central part. It could also be used to
describe our blood pump which is physical, or something physically
intangible, such as our feelings. We see an example of this in
Matthew.

Understanding the "Heart"

Spirit

Your born-again spirit is the heart of man. It is the core of who you are and operates in perfect knowledge regarding the things of God. These things can be revealed to your soul man when the mind is renewed to God's Word.

Inward
Man

Soul

Your soul is the heart of who you are in your mind, will and emotions and makes up your personality. It can operate with input from the physical body and when the spirit is born-again also can have deeper input from your spirit. By the free will that God gives each of us, the soul man ultimately decides our destiny in life by the choices it makes.

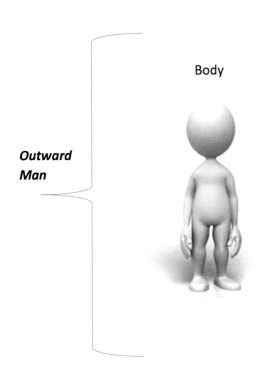

Body

Outward Man

Your body is only a copy or representation of what your spirit looks like and houses the physical heart. It gives you legal authority to operate on this earth and is dead without the spirit. However, our intellect and emotions, not being based on the physical body but the spirit, live on eternally in heaven or hell when the body dies.

"But those things that proceed out of the mouth, come forth from the heart; and they defile the man. (19) For out of the heart proceed evil thoughts, murders, adulteries, fornications, thefts, false witness, blasphemies." (Matthew 15:18-19)

Since your physical heart (blood pump) has no ability to think, the word heart in this context of scripture shows us that it is our thinking part or soul man. Our soul man is the gatekeeper of our mouth and decides what will be released. The context of this verse cannot be his own spirit because no negative thoughts originate here. This verse is referring to the heart of the mind. The heart of a man's mind could be defined as the predominant collective thoughts we have from life experiences stored in our brains. These thoughts are made up of how we perceive both natural and spiritual things as we renew our minds to the *world* or to the *Word*. Based on the amount of world or Word we have in us is a predicter of how we will respond and make decisions in life.

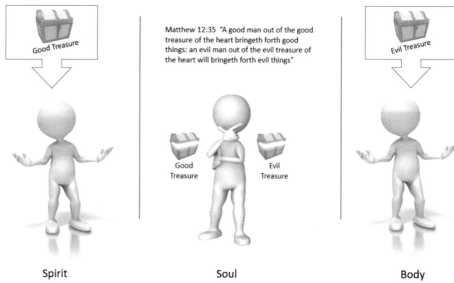

Spirit   Soul   Body

Being Led by the Spirit

From the time we are born, we generate thoughts and ideas from our experiences. God's will is that our thoughts would be framed around The Kingdom of God. The Kingdom God is His way of doing and being, unlike the Kingdom of Heaven, which is a place. We have two voices speaking to us: God through His Holy Spirit, and the voice of the world. The Holy Spirit's voice is the inner voice we have from God and is fed from our spirit man to our soul man.

Here is what this might look like:

- God speaks to the Holy Spirit
- The Holy Spirit speaks to our spirit man
- Our spirit man relays God's message to our soul man so that it may be digested and used (The catalyst for digestion is praying, meditating, and reading on The Word of God)
- When we read and meditate on The Word of God, our spirit man jumps in and bears witness to what we have just read and says to our soul, "We have a match!" In other words, what you just read is truth and life! Follow it!

If you think about this progression, it is the way our spirit man became born again. There is one important thing to point out here that cannot be missed. In Psalm 46:10 God says, "Be quiet and know that I am God."

God The Father

Wisdom

Wisdom

Wisdom

How does the Spirit of God Lead you?

Romans 8:15-16 says "For ye have not received the spirit of bondage again to fear, but ye have received the Spirit of Adoption whereby we cry Abba Father. The Spirit itself bare witness with our spirit, that we are the children of God.

Your Spirit, (with The Holy Spirit inside

Draw Wisdom from the Holy Spirit through your Spirit Man

John 16:13 Howbeit when He, The Spirit of Truth, is come, He will guide you into all truth; for He shall not speak of Himself; but whatsoever He shall hear, that He shall speak, and He will show your things to come.

Soul Man

The Word (Jesus)

"Be quiet and know that I am God." (Psalm 46:10)

The reason some do not hear from God is because they never get to a place where all other distractions or noises are turned off. This is explained in God's revelation to Elijah:

Then He said, "Go out, and stand on the mountain before the LORD." And behold, the LORD passed by, and a great and strong wind tore into the mountains and broke the rocks in pieces before the LORD, but the LORD was not in the wind; and after the wind an earthquake, but the LORD was not in the earthquake; and after the earthquake a fire, but the LORD was not in the fire; and after the fire a still small voice. (1 Kings 19:11-13) - NKJV

This verse from Elijah explains that the way to hear from God is to get still, remove distractions, and focus on Him. The way God spoke and created things in the beginning was not described as a still small voice. I imagine that when He said, "Let there be light" in Genesis 1:3, His voice shook the universe and would have obliterated us. Can you get a picture in your mind of God speaking to the sun? Great, then this book is starting to work, and you are seeing these images in your mind's eye!

You see, God's plan is that none should perish but all should come to the saving knowledge of Jesus Christ.

"The Lord is not slack concerning his promise, as some men count slackness; but is longsuffering to us-ward, not willing that any should perish, but that all should come to repentance." (2 Peter 3:9)

Although God's ultimate goal is that all His created children would accept Him as their Lord and Savior, unfortunately not all will. That is because He gave us something called free will so that we have the ability to choose. He chose not to create us as mindless robots and created us special and in His Image. Part of that image is the ability to choose for ourselves. God communicated in Deuteronomy that he set before all of us life and death. He loves us so much that He even gives the correct answer at the end of the verse.

"I call heaven and earth to record this day against you, that I have set before you life and death, blessing and cursing: therefore choose life, that both thou and thy seed may live." (Deuteronomy 30:19)

In school, I always liked the teachers who would not only tell us which questions were going to be on the test, but also reviewed the correct answers. If we were paying attention, we could certainly pass the test. Here God is doing the same thing and providing us the answer to life's most important question: "Will you choose me?" If you are not saved, is He speaking to you now?

Chapter 8

Facts vs Truths

To explain the title of this chapter, let us first look at the physical world that we all live in. You came into this physical world with a physical body from your mother's physical body. Your newly born physical body was cared for by your parents and was nurtured and fed. You advanced to crawling one day to walking and eventually to running. This progression was all physical. While all this was happening on the outside, there was also a change happening on the inside, meaning in your physical brain. Each day's experience led to another fact about the outside world that was quickly registered and stored away for the next experience to be added.

This constantly growing list of facts based on physical experiences and worldly teaching could be called your natural faith. Natural faith comes from two sources of input, your soul and body. We receive constant information daily form these two sources. We can touch someone's soul emotionally by the words we speak to them or we can touch someone's body physically with our hands. However, our spirit is not where our feelings are housed or can be touched physically. Look at the last part of 1 John 4:4, where it says, "…because greater is he that is in you, than he that is in the world." It could be difficult for you to understand this verse when facing a trial because you cannot feel your spirit where the Holy Spirit resides inside of you. You may feel like God is far away sometimes and all alone, but this could not be further from the truth! He is right there inside your spirit man, so you never have to pray, "Lord, please be with us."

Gravity teaches us that when we drop a ball, it falls to the ground. When we see a sturdy chair and sit down it supports our weight. Many people succeed in life based on this natural faith which produces many internal lists of past situations with probable outcomes. Natural faith comes from two sources of input, your soul and body. Were you aware that there is a real spiritual world that exists? In this realm there is also a supernatural faith that does not involve physical things that you can pick up with your natural senses. Let me explain.

There are **facts** in this world and there are **truths**. It seems that these two words, much like spirit and soul, are remarkably similar in people's minds and awfully close in terms of dictionary definitions. It may be a fact that the law of gravity is in operation here on the earth, but it is understood that this law can be overcome by a truth. When an airplane wing is forced through the air, other principles come into play such as lift, and the law of gravity is trumped. God is a spirit, and we must understand that not only is there is a physical world, but also a very real spiritual world.

Lift

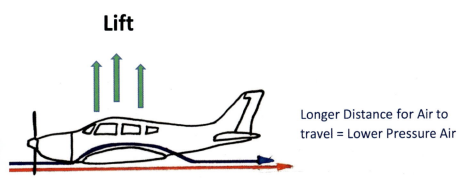

Longer Distance for Air to travel = Lower Pressure Air

Shorter Distance for Air to travel = Higher Pressure air to lift

While facts are all around us with the physical input that we experience though our five natural senses, there is spiritual dimension that exists as well where God has established spiritual principles or truths that operate without fail. Some would say that a truth is something that must be discovered to be real. This is not entirely correct. God's truths are real whether you discover them or not and exist with or without any exploration by you. They never have to be qualified by your own experience. But we must learn about them and understand that they are there.

If the devil can blind someone's eyes to the truth, then the second thing that can happen is that they harden their heart to the truth. "He hath blinded their eyes and hardened their heart; that they should not see with their eyes, nor understand with their heart, and be converted, and I should heal them." **(John 12:40)**

An atheist who possesses strong reasoning that God does not exist has convinced himself by means of his natural physical mind and has totally disallowed the understanding of spiritual things, including spiritual truths. This is his self-made reality and is very real to him. Let me give you an example that might help you more easily understand this principle.

Say you are driving down a road in an unfamiliar town and thinking about the place you are going, and suddenly you realize there are blue lights in your rear-view mirror. You pull over to the side of the road and wait for the officer to come to your door. The officer cautiously asks to see your driver's license and if you know why you were pulled over. You respond, "Not really," because your mind was somewhere else while you were driving. The officer tells you that you were exceeding the speed limit of 45 mph by 10 miles an hour and your response is, "I never saw the sign." The officer grins and says, "It is posted a couple of miles back and by the way, ignorance of the speed limit is no excuse for breaking the law."

Has this ever happened to you? The fact that you did not know or understand what the speed limit was, is no excuse for breaking it in the eyes of the officer or judge. No matter how hard you wanted to believe in your natural mind that the speed limit was 55 mph, the truth is, it is 45, and you are making a monetary donation that day!

Today we are seeing a migration to moral relativism where there is less black and white and more gray. Moral relativism is a viewpoint that moral judgments are true or false based on one's unique vantage point. When you make only your beliefs the benchmark for what is right or wrong instead of the Bible, you have no anchor for what truth is.

A growing number of people feel more comfortable with moral relativism because they can make up their own rules according to how they want to believe. Basically, their beliefs are based on how they feel and interpret their outside world. Over time we can develop harmful filters that block our understanding of a fact or a truth based on past experiences.

Man's religious filters

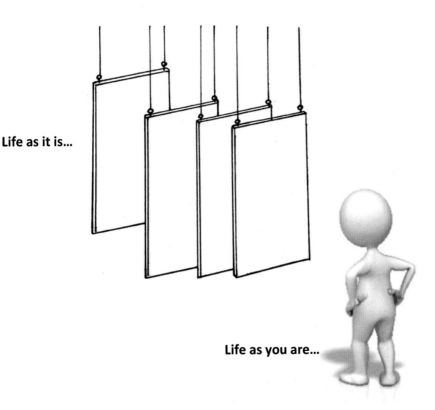

Life as it is...

Life as you are...

Religious filters can stack up before your eyes over time. They come from beliefs about God, based on wrong interpretations and influenced by the worldly knowledge instead of God's wisdom. Wrong beliefs are formed with a lack of understanding Biblical truths and based rather on man's opinions of assumed facts. If you do not read, all you know is what someone told you.

According to 1 Corinthians, we grow and mature, putting some things behind us. "When I was a child, I spake as a child, I understood as a child, I thought as a child: but when I became a man, I put away childish things." **(1 Corinthians 13:11)**

When we were a child, our views were narrower because of our limited perspectives on life. Just like camera film or a copying machine, our perspectives are developed by what our minds are *exposed* to. We develop only those things we see and hear. If we are exposed to the truths in God's Word, we will see life more clearly. However, if we are exposed to wrong beliefs and assumed facts that are incorrect, they will ultimately affect our actions in a negative way.

The next verse in 1 Corinthians says we view life through a glass darkly. The glass represents a mirror, but the mirror is a good distance away. The image reflected now is not entirely clear. As we expose our minds to God's Word, it is like walking closer to that mirror, and eventually it will lead us close enough that it will be like face to face.

"For now we see through a glass, darkly; but then face to face: now I know in part; but then shall I know even as also I am known."

(1 Corinthians 13:12)

The filter that we do need is found in **Philippians 4:8** which says:

"Finally, brethren, whatever is true, whatever is honorable, whatever is right, whatever is pure, whatever is lovely, whatever is of good repute, if there is any excellence and if anything worthy of praise, dwell on these things." In heaven, we will be able to interpret all things with perfect clarity.

Ignoring the Rules

Have you ever played a board or card game with someone who ignored the rules established by the maker or never took time to read how to play the game and made their own interpretation? You may have read the instructions and are trying hard to play by the rules, while others are breaking them. You can do one of two things: continue to play by the rules while at the same time enforcing them, or just adapt to theirs and continue.

Many times, if the world cannot remove the rule because it might be printed on a dollar bill or inscribed in granite on a government building, they will twist the original intent try to or make others look at it through their own filters. An example of this is how the devil twisted God's Word in the garden of Eden.

We use the term truth relativism to describe a condition where there are no absolute truths and what people believe is relative to some particular frame of understanding. All points of view are not equally valid, no matter how popular or trendy they may be. This kind of thinking has been the ruin of individuals and societies, as well as entire civilizations where essentially all moralities are believed to be equally good and belief systems equally true.

Just because you have no knowledge about a truth does not make it nonexistent or inoperative. Things such as radio waves exist in the room or place where you are reading this book, but you cannot see them. The same is true for God's truths. Understanding the truth about the three components that make up who you are will allow you to prosper in your spirit, soul, and body.

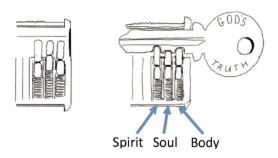

Spirit Soul Body

Just like a lock and key, when there is perfect alignment in your spirit, soul and body that comes from knowing God's truth. It is equivalent to having the authority to open and close the King's house as is mentioned in Isaiah. "And the key of the house of David will I lay upon his shoulder; so, he shall open, and none shall shut; and he shall shut, and none shall open." **(Isaiah 22:22)**

In ancient times, keys were quite large and carried on the shoulder. To display a key on your shoulder was a symbol of property or someone's trust, and a badge of authority. We see Eliakim the priest received the key to the house of David on his shoulder because he was a trusted servant.

God's Word will provide you the correct keys to His wisdom, truth, and knowledge. These are the keys to the kingdom!

Chapter 9

You Are a Free Agent!

I am not an avid movie goer, but I do find one now and then that interests me enough to go see. Of the ones I like the most, action movies are probably my favorites because they usually pit good against evil, and the good always wins! The movie *Braveheart* tells the story of the legendary Scottish hero William Wallace, played by Mel Gibson. Wallace leads the Scots against the English monarch Edward I, to fight for freedom from tyranny, and wins. In our own lives we need freedom from the tyranny of the devil, but our screenplay is much different in that the battle is the Lord's! We are required to show up for battle mentally prepared.

A verse that comes to mind is the 23rd Psalm. When the war is raging all around and you can feel the pressure of the attack, here is how God lays it out for us.

The LORD is my shepherd; I shall not want. He maketh me to lie down in green pastures: he leadeth me beside the still waters. He restoreth my soul: he leadeth me in the paths of righteousness for his name's sake. Yea, though I walk through the valley of the shadow of death, I will fear no evil: for thou art with me; thy rod and thy staff they comfort me. Thou preparest a table before me in the presence of mine enemies: thou anointest my head with oil; my cup runneth over. Surely goodness and mercy shall follow me all the days of my life: and I will dwell in the house of the LORD forever.
(Psalm 23:1-6)

Notice that when the attack comes, whether it is your health, your finances, a relationship, your future or your job, the Lord calmly sets up a table. He puts a white linen cloth over it and sets it up with the finest meal for the two you to dine on. Keep in mind that all this takes place here on Earth, because we have no enemies in heaven!

God then asks you, "What did you say you were afraid of?" Then, all your fears just dissolve as you experience His great love.

BREAKING NEWS

Life is a Choice! You are a FREE AGENT!

Feelings, nothing more than feelings….

Emotions have a purpose, but you cannot live a productive, fully satisfied life if you are living your life based solely on feelings. Someone once asked the well-known evangelist Billy Graham how he overcame fear and he responded, "I've read the last chapter of Revelation, and we win."

The end of the bible tells us, "We win!" Have you read that? You must understand that the good guy does win, and it is because he recognizes where his source comes from. If you are born again, you are members of God's army. No darkness can ever control light. If you were seated in a large auditorium in the upper seats and the power was turned off, you would be in darkness. Do you know it only takes a small match lit on the floor of that coliseum and anyone in that place can see light? Light dispels darkness; darkness does not dispel light!

Most likely you have never heard of someone afraid of the light, but there are plenty of people who are afraid of the dark, even into their adult years. Darkness must flee just like it had to in Genesis.

(Genesis 1:2-3)

"And the earth was without form, and void; and darkness was upon the face of the deep. And   the Spirit of God moved upon the face of the waters. And God said, Let there be light: and there was light." (Genesis 1:2-3)

In 1 John 1:5 we learn, "God is light, and in Him is *no* darkness *at all*". And we are in Him!   Remember that the battle is the Lord's.

"For though we walk in the flesh, we do not war after the flesh: (For the weapons of our warfare are not carnal but mighty through God to the pulling down of strong holds)" **(2 Corinthians 10:3-4)**

Rock, paper, scissors is a fun basic game of strategy in which one object has an advantage over another depending on what the opponent choses as a defense. Many practice rock, paper, scissors in their lives when it comes to defeating the devil. Sometimes you win and sometimes you lose, because it is all based on chance and is based on how you *feel*. Living by your feelings or being carnal is to give into bodily pleasures and appetites. We must never forget that we are free agents, and we have the ability to **choose**! The feelings you presently have are the ones that you have chosen. The key is remembering that the enemy has no power at all over us except what we give him. When we allow our natural or fleshly side to yield to fear or pride, then he can win. What it boils down to is this: are you going to sign for the package?

HUMAN EMOTIONAL LOVE VS GOD'S LOVE

Having unrighteous anger and a spirit of unforgiveness can lead to strife and is a direct path to getting out of our love walk. Picture in your mind for a moment that God's love is a curtain rod that everything else in your life hangs on. Your peace, joy, happiness, prosperity, healing, etc. When the commandment of love is violated in a situation, the spirit of fear is present, and your joy can be stolen.

Think of a recent situation when you allowed yourself to get away from your love walk. From the time a difficult person or situation presented itself, you had the unique ability that God gave us to "choose". You can decide and remain in control through the whole process if you are focused on who you are in your spirit where God resides. Perfect love is there all the time! Life is a choice, but many would rather allow their emotions and the devil to herd them into a corner where they feel trapped. As a result, they come out fighting.

If you listen carefully to the words people use in their discussions, you will learn a lot about where that person operates from, meaning from a spirit of faith or a spirit of fear. When people frequently overuse the word "feel", it indicates that they are more in touch with their flesh or body than they are with their spirit. Feelings do not make you who you are, they just reveal where your mind is trying to take you. They are operating in what this physical world has to offer in terms of direction. Most people are dominated by their five physical senses. Our five physical senses along and along with a remarkable brain to store our memories, recall past experiences to help shape future ones. That is when tragedy can strike. If we are accustomed to figuring things out in this manner, we will respond to fear or terror in the same way.

"For though we walk in the flesh, we do not war after the flesh; For the weapons of our warfare are not carnal, but mighty through God to pulling down of strong holds." **(2 Corinthians 10:3-4)**

God has formed in us a wonderful and perfect defense in the command, "Fear not, believe only." **(Luke 8:50)** First of all, it is not our job to fear, because this is one of satan's biggest weapons used against us. If he can get us to fear, then we are back to playing rock, paper, scissors with him again and whether we will be victorious is hit or miss. Remember, you have been given the right to choose where your mind goes!

Chapter 10

Are You Still Growing?

An old adage says, "Many people die at twenty-five and aren't buried until they are seventy-five." The meaning here is that when people quit reading, learning, or growing, they are done inside their minds. "My people are destroyed for lack of knowledge..." **(Hosea 4:6)** If you do not read, all you know is what someone told you. How sad is that? For this reason, it is so important to regularly read the Bible for yourself.

Attending a church that is not vibrant and growing has a way of preconditioning you to a vague set of rules. When rules are the focus, it is called religion. Sermon after sermon and lesson after lesson begin to crystalize in your mind an image of who God is. Is your image of God one of anger, vengeance, and wrath? If so, you may begin thinking of what you can do to satisfy God and win His approval. Walking away from the worship experience may lead you to think, "If I am this bad, why even try to improve?"

I can remember talking with my uncle about God when he was in his fifties. Several times I invited him to church with me and one day he told me that a house of hypocrites was not his thing. He went out on weekends and saw how the so-called church goers or goody-two shoes who were in church on Sunday had acted the night before when he was partying with them. He decided that he could be a much better person if he never darkened the doorstep of any church. "Besides, when you went, all they did was condemn you. Where's the fun in that?" he asked.

Learning is for a lifetime...

It seems some in life never really "grow up" and continue to stay in a childlike state when it comes to deeper learning. They will learn more if it is fun, but if there is any work involved, they lose interest quickly.

In a child's earlier years of using pen and paper, two and three-year-olds begin to scribble. There is no effort to draw a picture but is really more of an exercise of play, motor skills, and the desire to create that God put into each of us. As a child turns four or five, they identify that circles represent people's heads and that lines equate to legs and arms.

If asked, most children over the age of six can easily identify many shapes like squares, triangles and circles. However, three-dimensional shapes are not as easily understood. Although we live in a 3-D world, how many of us could understand how to draw a 3-D picture of something?

As they progress to the eight to twelve-year-old stage of drawing, children become aware of spatial differences and three-dimensional depiction of objects and become more critical of trying to draw things as they actually appear. Lastly, by the time they reach their teenage years, many realize that art is just not something for them, and any further development in their abilities to draw realistically ceases. Why? They stopped growing in this area.

Our growth in the Word of God is similar, because anything that is growing bears fruit, and anything that stops growing dies. I heard a speaker many years ago make this comment, "We should all be like **green tomatoes** because when you see a green tomato, you know it is still growing." When people begin to think that they already know everything about a subject and stop growing, the result is like a rotting tomato. They begin to stink! Colossians speaks to why we should continue to grow.

That ye might walk worthy of the Lord unto all pleasing, being fruitful in every good work, and increasing in knowledge of God; Strengthened with all might, according to his glorious power, unto all patience and longsuffering with joyfulness; Giving thanks unto the Father, which hath made us meet to be partakers of the inheritance of the saints in light. **(Colossians 1:10-12)**

As we become adults, many of us stop growing in different areas of God's Word. We may be like the adolescent who struggles to understand how to draw a realistic picture and stops because it may be difficult to learn. It seems that when we come across an area in God's Word that does not line up with our previous learning, we stop trying to understand. When it comes to understanding more about how God relates to us, it is a tremendous help to understand how He originally made us: spirit, soul, and body.

I have found a much deeper understanding of God's Word through the study of spirit, soul, and body. I believe that you will begin to see your identity in Christ more clearly when you understand that there was so much more that changed when you were saved than your eternal destination or shipping orders.

Spiritual growth occurs when the believer is transformed by the renewing of the mind. Renewing of your mind happens in direct proportion to the extent that it is daily exposed to the Word of God. Without action, your mind won't stay renewed any more than your hair combed.

It is one thing to look *at* God's Word, but it is quite another to look *into* God's Word. When walking through a bookstore you may get excited about the title of a book you see, but unless you open that book and look *into* its contents, all you have is a little exuberance. I can relate, because many of us who like to read will walk slowly through a bookstore aisle, scanning the titles that seem interesting. But unless we pick it up and investigate it, the best title in the world will do you no good, even if it is the Bible! It is like window shopping without going into the store to really check it out. An overwhelming number of people live their lives window shopping the Word of God and wonder why they don't understand how to receive their peace, joy, healing, prosperity, favor, and on, and on.

The same outcome may happen when we look for a church to attend. We must go beyond window shopping or judging churches by how they look on the outside; we must check them out on the inside. Unfortunately, some choose their churches the same way they choose their clothes; they make decisions based on what is in fashion at the moment. By the way, the closest church in proximity to where you live may not be the church you need to attend for growth in your spiritual walk. How far down the road would we get in our car if we choose the water hose because it was closer than the fuel pump?

Without checking into what that a church believes, you may be hampering your spiritual growth. A church that is only focused on truth without grace will be mean spirited. Truth without grace beats people up because it lacks love. A church that is mainly focused on grace with little or no truth, lacks honesty. Grace without truth chooses not to confront sin and makes being nice the goal instead of being real. Jesus always balances truth with grace and the church you are planted in should do likewise so that you may grow in truth and knowledge of God's Word.

Chapter 11

"Walk this way, talk this way…"

I grew up with the understanding that we needed to let Jesus save our soul. When Ephesians says to put on the new man, it means that something has changed. "And that ye put on the new man, which after God is created in righteousness and true holiness." **(Ephesians 4:24)**

What really happened? Who got saved? How would you explain this experience to someone who is not saved? When we experience receiving Jesus as our Lord and Savior, we indeed become a brand-new person in our spirit. So, what happened to the old one? Did he evaporate?

A suit of clothes is to the body as the body is to your spirit and soul. Would you agree that when putting on a new suit of clothes would renew the attitude of your mind or change the way you walk? Are there certain things you would not think about doing like giving your dog a bath in a new suit? When you put on the new man, you allow the Spirit of God inside your spirit man to change the attitude of your mind in your soul man. Incrementally you would change some of the activities you used to do.

Your spirit can do without your body, but your body cannot do without your spirit. You may think of your body as an earth suit or as a tank that provides mobility and the legal right to operate here. The devil has no body and therefore no legal right to operate here, so he is limited to only working through willing people.

I could understand what it was like to put on new clothes, but what was the new man? When you understand that you are a spirit, that you have a soul, and that you live in a body, you have an exciting life changing revelation! 1 John states, we become just like God on the inside: holy, pure, loving, and good. We now have the ability to be truly victorious in this world!

"Herein is our love made perfect, that we may have boldness in the day of judgment: because as he is, so are we in this world." **(1 John 4:17)**

The whole process is an inside job, meaning that God changes you from the inside out. You were given a new spirit, not a new soul. We must allow that new spirit man to manifest on the outside, so we make right decisions in our soul man.

We do that by renewing our minds to what the Word says about us and by getting in agreement with it and acting on it. "And be not conformed to this world: but be ye transformed by the renewing of your mind, that ye may prove what *is* that good, and acceptable, and perfect, will of God." **(Romans 12:2)** If it were our souls that got saved, there would be no reason or justification to renew our minds because they would be already just like God's.

Ephesians 5:1 tells us to walk and talk like God. "Therefore be imitators of God, as beloved children." (English Standard Version) To be imitators we must talk like Him and walk like Him. When we become reborn in our spirit, we can imitate God and he even gives us other examples to encourage us:

- "Be perfect, therefore, as your Heavenly Father is perfect." (Matthew 5:48)
- "Be merciful, just as your Father is merciful." (Luke 6:36)

- "And be ye kind one to another, tenderhearted, forgiving one another, even as God for Christ's sake hath forgiven you. (Ephesians 4:32)
- "That ye may be blameless and harmless, the sons of God, without rebuke, in the midst of a crooked and perverse nation, among whom ye shine as lights in the world;" (Philippians 2:15)

It is interesting to see the resemblance that children have to their fathers and mothers. Some of the most noticeable are the ways we speak and how we pronounce words in the same way as our parents. Often, we even subliminally watch and imitate our parents in the ways they walk or stand. Just as how you are raised in your family and begin to pick up or imitate the actions of your parents, once we are born again, we begin to imitate the actions of our heavenly Father.

Think, Talk, and then Walk!

As you spend time in God's Word and hear His voice, His nature becomes more real to you and you begin to follow that up by how you think. Your thoughts lead to beliefs, your beliefs lead to actions and your actions lead to a new walk or way of life. Galatians 5:16 says, "Walk in the Spirit, and ye shall not fulfil the lust of the flesh." The default position we are born with is death; however, a newborn Christian's disposition is life! As your minds are renewed to His way of thinking, we may begin to trump the desires of the flesh and walk in the fruit of the spirit after our Lord.

This starts first by changing how we think. "As a man believes in his heart, so is he" **(Proverbs 23:7)** God never does anything without saying it first. In Matthew 16:19 Jesus said, "I give you the keys of the kingdom, whatever you bind on earth will be bound in heaven, whatever you loose on earth will be loosed in heaven." This means you can speak the Word and bind evil from you here, because evil is bound in heaven. Conversely, you can also speak the Word and loose those things here that are allowed in heaven. God's Word is first in our spirits, and then released in the form of our words to have power over evil or release good into our lives. In addition, you have been given the power of attorney that enables you to use the mighty name of Jesus as the enforcer.

Just like words are important in a court of law, words are extremely important to God. "...God, who quickeneth the dead, and calleth those things which be not as though they were." **(Romans 4:17)** Here God is telling us in another way that life and death are in the power of the tongue. Look at Proverbs 14:3: "In the mouth of the foolish is the rod of pride: but the lips of the wise will preserve them." When we speak God's words over our situation it preserves us from the enemy who wants to steal, kill, and destroy us. The lesson here on how we talk is that the lips of the wise will preserve us from the enemy.

Once we are born again, we become one-third like God, meaning that our spirit man is sanctified and is now made 100% righteous just like Jesus! On the other hand, our soul and body are waiting to be 100% redeemed and having our final home in heaven as the time draws near to Jesus's return.

Spotless Church

For the longest time I wondered how God could come back for a spotless church. I did not understand what it meant to be the righteousness of Christ in Jesus; now I know! Those who are saved are made completely spotless in their spirit man, waiting for the soul and body to be fully redeemed in the last days. Our souls are renewed daily as we continue in the Word of God and is an ongoing process until we die or are raptured.

Behold, I tell you a mystery; We shall not all sleep, but we shall all be changed, in a moment, in the twinkling of an eye, at the last trump: for the trumpet shall sound, and the dead shall be raised incorruptible, and we shall be changed. For this corruptible must put on incorruption, and this mortal must put on immortality. So when this corruption shall have put on incorruption, and this mortal shall have put on immortality, then shall be brought to pass the saying that is written, Death is swallowed up in victory. O death, where is thy sting? O grave, where is thy victory? The sting of death is sin; and the strength of sin is the law. But thanks be to

God, which giveth us the victory through our Lord Jesus Christ. **(1 Corinthians 15:51-57)**

These verses explain to us at the rapture when our soul and new body are finally made 100% like Jesus at the rapture in the twinkling of an eye! Those who are dead in Christ will be raised first and then those who are alive will be caught up in the air to be with Him together forever! Our new resurrected bodies will be like Jesus' body. It can be touched but with a new dimension to it that never tires, gets old, weak, or sick. You will not even gain weight!

Let us remember John 4:17: "As He is, so are we in this world." Romans tells us that Jesus was the *firstborn among many brethren*. "For whom he did foreknow, he also did predestinate to be conformed to the image of his Son, that he might be the firstborn among many brethren." **(Romans 8:29)** God will have a church that is conformed to the image of his Son.

Chapter 12

The Gift of Faith

If Jesus's faith worked better than yours, wouldn't you want a measure of His? The good news is that He gives us His faith. Here is how He does this: "So then faith cometh by hearing and hearing by the Word of God." **(Romans 10:17)** Hearing all by itself does not mean that you receive salvation, but faith in what Jesus accomplished on the cross does.

God is no respecter of persons, meaning that the floor before the altar of almighty God is level, and that each one standing before Him has no advantage over another. Unlike what you may have experienced with your parents or grandparents here on earth, He looks out at all his children and loves them equally with no partiality or favorites. Since He is no respecter of persons, He gives to each of us *the same* measure of faith. What we do with that measure determines who we become and the things that we accomplish while we are on this earth.

"For I say, through the grace given unto me, to every man that is among you, not to think of himself more highly than the ought to think; but to think soberly, according as God hath dealt to every man the same measure of faith." **(Romans 12:3)**

Notice that God did not say He hath dealt to every man *a* measure of faith. The word "a" and the phrase, "*a measure*" in this sentence are adjectives. As we know from early schooling, an adjective is a word or phrase naming an attribute, quantity, or further description of a noun or pronoun. What is especially interesting about *a* vs *the* is that these words are also known as articles. An article is always used with a noun to indicate the type of reference being made by the noun. They fall into two categories, which are definite and indefinite.

Articles

Definite article example: the

Indefinite article example: a, an

The definite article *the* is used when people are describing something in particular or more specific.

The indefinite article *a* and *an* are used when people are describing something general.

When God used the definite article *the*, He meant something extremely specific and not just any measure but *the* particular measure. If it were *a* measure, this could mean that some people may have received a different amount than from others. This would undermine the belief that God is no respecter of persons. It may appear that someone else may have more faith than you do, but it is only that they are using more of their faith than you may be.

How do you use *the* measure of faith?

When you come across what may seem in the physical to be an impossible problem, faith kicks in and says that it is possible. "Now faith is the substance of things hoped for, the evidence of things not seen." **(Hebrew 1:11)** Notice that this verse starts off with the word now. Faith is always in the present tense. With God there is no future and no past because time only exists in the physical realm. Since we live in this world where time does exist, there are occasions when it takes time for the manifestation of what your earnestly prayed for and released with your faith. Hope is for the future and is like a goal setter until faith manifests. It is like you walking to your home thermostat and dialing in 70 degrees when it is only 60 degrees in the house. You are practicing Romans 4:17 by calling those things that are not as though they are, and you may not even realize it.

God talking to Abraham: "As it is written, I have made thee a father of many nations, before him whom he believed, *even* God, who quickeneth the dead, and calleth those things which be not as though they were." **(Romans 4:17)**

If your soul is influenced by your body and the world around you, doubt will erode your prayer of faith. Do not bend to the pressure of time; fear not and believe only. Galatians 6:9 says, "And let us not grow weary in well doing for in due season we will reap, if we faint not."

Body   Soul   Spirit

Raise your hope to give you something to hang your faith on. Lift your head and get excited that the victory is yours! God is your high tower, deliverer, and comforter. Nothing is impossible with God!

Faith + Hope + Love

NKJV "And now abide faith, hope, love, these three; but the greatest of these *is* love." (**1 Corinthians 13:13**)

If your soul is influenced by your spirit and the things of God, faith along with hope, will be there. You do not need to try to get more faith; you just need to release the measure of faith that God has already given you in your spirit man with your words. Real faith always has a corresponding action. You are pregnant with faith in your spirit. A woman is either pregnant or she is not, and the same can be said of our faith. A pregnant woman does not have levels of pregnancy, she only has the manifestation of what is already there! We give birth to things in our lives by the words we speak in faith or in fear.

The Catalyst of Faith is Love

Although you may be in faith and expectant of an answered prayer, it cannot work where there is an absence of love. Galatians 5:6 says, "Faith worketh by love." Since faith is a byproduct of love, we can check our love walk toward others to monitor if we are operating in faith. It starts out with showing our genuine love for God by our obedience to Him. Secondly, we have kind actions toward others that are not works of the law, but out of genuine love for one another. Love is the curtain rod that all the promises of God hang on. If you think about it, to walk in love toward others you must have your spirit, soul and body all working together with the spirit man taking the lead like the picture above.

If you are truly walking in love toward others, you will also forgive them. Is there anyone in your mind right now that immediately pops up that you have not completely forgiven? In Luke 17, Jesus taught:

If your brother or sister sins against you, rebuke them; and if they repent, forgive them. Even if they sin against you seven times in a day and seven times come back to you saying I repent, you must forgive them. The apostles said to the Lord, "Increase our faith!" He replied, "If you have faith as small as a mustard seed, you can say to this mulberry tree, 'Be uprooted and planted in the sea,' and it will obey you." (Luke 17: 3-4)

The Progression of Faith

- Hearing – Brings to your mind the will of God delivered in His Word
- Faith generates in our spirit as a result or outcome of hearing the will of God.

- Hope builds as the goal setter of what you can receive, is generated in your spirit man, and is then transferred to your soul man.
- The soul man begins processing hope and faith by either accepting them as truth or by doubting them based on the five senses, recalled memories, and past experiences.
- If the truth you now have is overruled by any of your five senses or negative recalled experiences, your outcome is doubt. In this case your belief is cancelled out, leaving you with only hope again.

"Hope deferred makes the heart sick…" **(Proverbs 13:12)** You know that God *can*, but now you are unsure if God *will*. The truth is, if it is a promise from God in His Word, He already has already granted it.

- Your only real mission left, is getting to the point of belief where you will receive spiritually first, so the answer may manifest in your soul (mind), and ultimately in your physical body.

There are two places of Faith

> But the righteousness which is of faith speaketh on this wise…but what saith it? The Word is nigh thee, even in thy mouth, and in thy heart; that is, the Word of Faith which we preach; that if thou shall confess with the mouth the Lord Jesus, and shall believe in thine heart that God hath raised Him from the dead, thou shall be saved. *(Romans 10:6-9)*

The Word is first in your spirit, then confessed with your mouth, and then it enters into your heart. You give birth to it by confessing with your tongue.

Let me give you an example.

I had taken my two sons on vacation to Yellowstone National Park for our first snowmobile trip. When got we got checked out on the snowmobiles we had rented, one of the pieces of advice given by the instructor was to stay on the main trails for safety and because you would miles away from any help.

After we had been riding for several hours on the trails, we all decided to pull over and have some lunch. We were in a valley area that had a long plain of beautiful pristine deep snow between two hills. After we had finished eating, my younger son started up his snowmobile, looked at that long plain of snow and back again to us to announce, "I'm going for it." He was doing great and was quickly out of sight to a point that we could no longer hear his engine running. We called out to him a couple of times and then he returned with, "I'm stuck!"

With every step we took to rescue him, our legs sank down three to four feet. When we finally managed to reach him, we were about 300 yards away from the trail. In slowing to make a turn and head back to the trail, his snowmobile plunged completely under the six-foot-deep snow like quicksand and was completely buried. Since this was the first time any of us had ridden snowmobiles, we did not know the tricks of getting out if you were stuck and did not even have a shovel. The situation looked hopeless in the physical, and doubt tried to enter our minds.

We all paused, said a prayer believing God would give us wisdom and the ability to get unstuck since we were about 25 miles away from any outside help.

After praying in faith, ideas started to come. Before an hour had passed, we were successful in getting the snowmobile dug out with our hands and had patted down the snow to for a makeshift ramp to launch it back out of the deep crater in the snow.

It was a celebration to get out of what looked like an impossible situation! Days after the trip as I was thinking about the experience, it occurred to me that someone else with knowledge of how to get unstuck in a situation like this may not call it faith at all because they already knew how to accomplish this from seeing someone else do it.

That, my friends, is called natural faith or learned faith in the physical world. The main point to this story is that when you do not have all the answers, consider God first and turn over your cares to our heavenly Father. You connect to Him through your spirit and soul, not your soul and body. Whether it is a serious health challenge or possibly a financial setback, He can help you take your impossible situation to a possible one in every area of your life.

There are way more things in life for which we do not know the answers than those for which we do. Even the people you know (or know of) who seem like they have all the answers, do not. We are forever limited on our own, but we are limitless and powerful with a relationship with our loving God and Creator.

Time to Realize What You Have

One must go from believing to perceiving. "Nay, in all these things we are more than conquerors through him that loved us. **(Romans 8:37)** The last thing that the devil wants you to know is that you are a new creation made 100% righteous in the eyes of God. When you know you are righteous, it is much easier to live in righteousness. See yourself the way God sees the real you in our spirit man being victorious in all things.

The Bible calls us kings and priests. "And hath made us kings and priests unto God and his Father; to him be glory and dominion for ever and ever. Amen." **(Revelation 1:6)** We are also called world overcomers: "For whatsoever is born of God overcometh the world: and this is the victory that overcometh the world, even our faith." **(1 John 5:4).**

But you my say, "I don't feel victorious or like a conqueror." Faith is not a feeling; it is a reality and a truth when you accept it into your heart. We do not feel our way into acting, we act our way into feeling. Believe and act on the truth letting your feelings just catch up. There are no failures in the covenant of God, only undeveloped skills in knowing you are the righteousness of God by faith through Jesus. You cannot believe any further than you have knowledge.

"Grace and peace be multiplied unto you through the knowledge of God, and of Jesus our Lord, According as his divine power hath given unto us all things that pertain unto life and godliness, through the knowledge of him that hath called us to glory and virtue:" **(II Peter 1:2-3)**

But now you have more knowledge! Learn to never let your feelings take the driver's seat in life because they will always lead you into a ditch. Scripture will keep you from making purely emotional decisions with the balance of rational thinking. Walk in the spirit and you will succeed to greater heights than you could have ever expected.

You can now break free from areas of your life where their exists defeat, discouragement, and dismay. Instead, you can grow in the Lord with a fresh revelation of who you are in Christ. Problems that seemed to be mountains in your life can become speed bumps. This newness of life can begin when we see ourselves through the eyes of a loving, Heavenly Father!

When your soul man makes the decision to agree with your spirit or inner man, you choose righteousness and the majority rules! Renewing your mind daily and agreeing with your spirit releases the whole backpack of blessings to you. We should live out of our spirit man which holds blessing and righteousness, instead of the default of living out of our body, which holds onto position and emotions. Only then will we enjoy the ability to stand in the presence of holy God without the feeling of guilt, inferiority, or unworthiness.

As you are about to finish this book, my hope is that you understand the things you have been trying to get from God, you already have. We must receive the benefits of what He has already done for us through His son. You were transformed and became a child of God when you were saved and became a joint heir with Jesus now, not later. Life should be enjoyed, not endured!

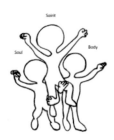

Which way are you leaning now?

Friend, do you want to start living the abundant life that your loving heavenly Father desires for you to have? God wants you to understand that the law of the old covenant makes you conscious of your soul and body. Focusing who we are in our imperfect souls and bodies only reminds us of our regrets, failures, and shortcomings. But understanding the grace of the New Covenant and asking Jesus to be the Lord of your life, makes you aware of his love for you, by the price he paid on the cross. You now become conscious of who you are in your spirit man fully accepted by God our Father.

And when you accept Jesus as your Lord and savior, God looks at your reborn spirit man and he sees Jesus! Your physically alive body is the temporary place holder in this life, providing you ultimately only two options. You have the free will that God gave you to accept and receive his son Jesus's perfect test score for your life and eternal salvation in Heaven or reject him and receive a real and eternal hell. Once the body dies, judgment comes without any chance to be saved later. Matthew 5:8 says, "Blessed are the pure in heart: for they shall see God." The word "blessed" here means only those who have accepted Jesus into their hearts shall see eternal salvation in heaven.

Christianity is not another religion. It is an actual relationship with God, possible through his precious Son named Jesus, living, and growing like a seed. This seed is in the form of the Holy Spirit and resides in the spirit man of every born-again believer. God is patient with his promises toward us, and he desires that no one should perish or be lost.

Has this book opened the eyes of your understanding of just how much God loves you? Are you just tired of trying to shoulder the problems in your life all alone? Are you like the prodigal son who experienced loneliness, hopeless and desperation? Have you been trying to handle the problems in your life all alone?

Like the prodigal son, you can also make the decision to come back to a Father who has his arms open wide for you: a loving heavenly Father who wants to give you his acceptance, love and forgiveness through grace, a Father who is no longer mad at you, but madly in LOVE with you!

Compared to eternity, our time on this planet is only a vapor. There are no dress rehearsals in life, and you have only one opportunity while you are here to make the right decision. The good news is that if you are reading this book, you still have the opportunity to make a decision for Jesus *today*!

If you would like to receive all that Jesus has done for you, and make him your Lord and Savior, please pray this prayer from your heart:

"Father God, I come to you now. Sin, I turn my back on you. Jesus, I turn to you now. I believe you died on the cross just for me. I believe you were raised from the dead just for me. Come into my spirit and be my Lord. I surrender my life to you today. I enter into relationship with you today, in Jesus's name, Amen."

We Would Like to Hear from You!

If you just prayed the salvation prayer, or if you have a testimony to share after reading this book, please contact us and let us know. We would like to give you (free of charge) a small witnessing tool to let others also know who they are in Christ: Spirit, Soul and Body. Contact us at: urspiritsoulbody@gmail.com

Acknowledgements

There have been many instrumental people in my life whose love, insight and encouragement have been extremely important in the creation of this book. While there are too many to mention here, I would like to give special recognition to a few.

To my Lord and Savior Jesus Christ, thank you for your grace and knowledge that have been poured into me through your precious Holy Spirit to pen the words of this book and an ability to draw. I pray that the words and ideas you have given me and expressed in this book about your love and plan for our lives with you will lead countless others to give their lives to you or bring those that already know you into a closer relationship with You!

To my precious Proverbs 31 wife and best friend, thank you for the love and inspiration you continually pour into me through your sweet spirit! From reading early drafts to giving me advice on the cover, you are a part of this book. You give testimony to Proverbs 18:22 that says, "He who finds a wife finds a good thing and obtains favor from the Lord." You are my GOOD THING!

To my three amazing children Taylor, Conner, and Cara, whom God has used to teach me so much about His love and laughter. The family unit is one of God's best ideas and creations. I am so thankful to understand firsthand the blessing of children, and proud of each of you and your spouses for keeping Him first in all that you do.

To my spiritual father, mentor and pastor, Jim Frease, whose straightforward and bold teaching of God's Word has propelled me and my family to greater heights. Your visionary leadership and accomplishments have inspired me and countless others, more than you realize this side of heaven.

To a close friend and brother in Christ, Jim Lanier, who constantly encouraged me during the writing of this book, even though it took many years to finally complete. Thank you for your patient continued support and for asking me the question one day, "How will you know when your book is finished?" I enjoyed the time with

God so much in writing the book, that I needed the extra push to tell me it was time to publish and share with others.

To my friend Ameillia Bozeman, for the time and effort you gave to editing my book. I thank you and Randy for your long friendship and being an inspiration to our family all these years.

To the millions of people in this world who are searching for the understanding of just how much God loves you and how he passionately wants you to know his son Jesus. Once you understand who you are in Christ, your world will change forever!

References

Chapter 2

1* Dake Publishing, Inc., "Dake's Annotated Reference Bible", Genesis 2:7, Footnote "Y", pg 3

2* Dake Publishing, Inc., "Dake's Annotated Reference Bible", Genesis 2:7, Footnote "C", pg 3

Chapter 3

1* Based on quote from Pastor Jim Frease, Joy Church International, "God is no longer mad at us…. He is madly in Love with us!

2* Based on quote from Pastor Jim Freese, Joy Church International, "Winning with Wisdom" book- "Pearls of Wisdom for your Next Right Decision", Vol 3 pages (187 & 188)

Chapter 4

1* Based on quote from Pastor Jim Freese, Joy Church International, "God is not a car-wrecking, cancer causing Creator. He is a loving Heavenly Father! God is not mad at you; He is madly IN LOVE WITH YOU!"

2* Based on quote from Pastor Jim Freese, Joy Church International, "Winning with Wisdom" book, Vol. 2 pg 178, "God's love is never based on the character of the receiver. God's love is based on the character of the Giver".

Chapter 5

1* Based on information from Healing Room Ministries, The Law of Life and Law of Death", John G. Lake, available from http://healingrooms.com

2* Based on quote from Pastor Jim Freese, Joy Church International, "There will come a time in your life that all you have left is what you have given to The Lord."

Chapter 7

2* Mai-Ly N. Steers, Robert E. Wickham, and Linda K. Acitelli (2014). Seeing Everyone Else's Highlight Reels: How Facebook Usage is Linked to Depressive Symptoms. Journal of Social and Clinical Psychology: Vol. 33, No. 8, pp. 701-731. https://doi.org/10.1521/jscp.2014.33.8.701

3* Based on quote from Pastor Jim Freese, Joy Church International, "There will come a time in your life that all you have left is what you have given to The Lord."

Made in the USA
Monee, IL
27 May 2021

69628741R00071